MISS MAI
...a love story

by Lewis MacLeod

1
What Happened to Me Forty Years Ago

When I was twenty-four years old, I fell in love.

Who doesn't, at such an age? But for me, the doing of it…it took me by surprise. No, that's not right. It took me by <u>storm</u>, the way the Mongols took an innocent, peaceable, defenseless market-town in the thirteenth century. No mercy…resistance was futile. Love pincushioned me with her arrows. Love's sickle-bladed shortswords skewered my heart, slashed through my liver and lights. Love trampled me under two thousand iron-shod hooves. Love grabbed me by my scalp and shook me around and body-slammed me onto stony, dry ground a half dozen times. Love hanged me on an iron derrick over seething coals and left me to roast.

I would go back and let all that happen again if only I could.

I barely survived all that and I have never been the same person since all those things happened to me. As of today that was more than forty years ago. I am not over it yet. I doubt I ever will be, as long as I might live. This is the way love ought to be.

Up until now, I've pretty much kept all this to myself. But I'll tell you about it if you like.

2

I Endure an Awkward Youth and Several Rocky Romances

I was a soldier. Before that, I was a university undergraduate. Even earlier, I was an adolescent, a public-school student. Whatever my scholarly merits as a student, I was not very impressive as a boy, once adolescence set in. Not particularly athletic, rather average-looking. Maybe even less-than-average. Big goggly glasses. Not a sharp dresser. Awkward and inarticulate. Indecipherable sense of the absurd. Just as important perhaps: NOT the offspring of wealthy or renowned parents. My dad was an engineer of such arcane brilliance that his intellect probably scared people…certainly, he horrified all my peers and struck them with awe. A small, illustrative anecdote: I remember him trying to describe a mathematical algorithm to me that used complex numbers to conceptualize the movement of pressure waves across the interface between two elastic mediums (are you with me so far???) I pointed to an expression in the computer code he was waving about. "What's rho-sub-sigma?" I asked him. He'd spelled it 'Rhosigma' in his computer code. He would have typed it using Greek letters if he could have figured out how. "That's the density in grams per cubic centimeter of the solid medium at a gas-solid interface," he casually replied. "Well why don't you name the variable 'solid_medium_density' in your source-code? Then everybody would know what you're talking about," I asked him, me always being a big fan of computer mnemonics that actually mean something, and never afraid of a little extra typing. "Um…er…<u>EVERYbody</u> knows what rho-sub-sigma is!!" my dad replied. So arcanely brilliant that he was clueless, that man! My mom was the girl's athletic-department director at the local high school, and was a veritable force of nature. My older brother had ceaselessly tornadoed a path of intellectual mayhem through school a year ahead of me, leaving the detritus of his passing for me to live down. The upshot was, when I started developing an interest in girls, I labored beneath the weight of such burdens that it did not work out so well for me.

Today's television fare lays it out so clearly: in order for girls to pay attention to you, young men, you'd better be slim, blond, clear-skinned, athletic, well-dressed, and sprung from well-to-do parents. Little else matters. Starting at about age twelve. In fact, if you are also disdainful of authority, smartmouthed, noncooperative in the matter of schoolwork (or a trifle stupid, even!), a "bad" boy by many measures, all that is to the good when it comes to impressing the girls. By the lights of modern popular literature, it seems to help if you are a vampire, or maybe a werewolf. With exemplars like that, I was going nowhere with the young ladies of my acquaintance. My earliest forays into romance went spectacularly unrequited. It was a constant source of teenage pain for me.

Well then one day when I was sixteen or so there was this girl who was a year younger and two classes behind me, who had come up through the elementary grades hearing of ME! Seems as if one of her favorite teachers, back at the old grammar-school, had sometimes bandied my name about as a citeable role-model: "Why can't you kids be more like my former student, who could – " etcetera, etcetera. For the first half of her frosh year, this little blonde angel opened her hallway locker directly above my own, banged my head every so often with the locker-door, but gently, then swapped out her books and papers, slammed the locker closed, and never uttered a word to me. All the while, a shy little crush developed on her part. Then one day, it happened that we got to talking! To each other! It was nice! For the first time in my life, there was a girl, undeniably cute, who LIKED ME BACK! We were destined to become high-school sweethearts (cue the sappy love-song, deejay!)

Unfortunately, her mother did not like me at all. It took me a long time to figure out why. In my ardent belief, it was because her mother was trying to re-live and improve upon her own miserable teenage high school years vicariously through her daughter, and I was nowhere near the mental image she had of 'boyfriend'. Look back at that laundry-list of my character flaws: I needed to have been a lettered Baseball Hero, president of the

3

student body, and firstborn scion of a wealthy family…perhaps the son of a bank official or a successful real-estate developer. And I certainly ought to have been the child of a conservative, pious, church deacon and/or conservative, pious upscale Country-Club resident-member. I needed to have manifested an insouciant The-devil-may-care-but-I-certainly-don't attitude, displayed a pearly-toothed, killer smile, had fiendish good looks and a well-groomed mop of gold-blond hair to have been good enough to have been acceptable as Mrs. Girlfriend's-Mom's only-child's high-school boyfriend. Well I was none of these, so Mrs. Girlfriend's-Mom disapproved. Worse than disapproved…*loathed* me! Loathed the very idea of me. I had never had an adult person take any kind of particular dislike to me, ever before, and it kinda hurt! Since Mrs. G-M micromanaged my little blonde angel's entire range of doings, I was forbidden to date her. She was forbidden to so much as speak to me.

So we engaged in Forbidden Love. It wasn't easy. No dates. No furtive afterschool trysts. No Saturday rendezvous at the mall. No wearing of exchanged Class Rings. Giving Christmas presents was a tricky business. Enrolling in A Capella Choir together, as we did one year, was seriously pushing the envelope, and I learned much later that my little blonde angel's mom had considered moving her to another school over that one. A private all-girl's school, with uniforms and exceptionally mean overseers. Extracurricularly speaking, Mrs. Girlfriend's-Mom could offer no sane objection (although it made her gnash her teeth fiercely!) if every Sunday I attended the same church services as my blonde angel, and so I did. Suited up – coat and tie – and drove myself to the 9 a.m. service at the Lutheran Church, for nearly a year. For all the good it did me. Had to sit a couple pews back, and couldn't talk to her before or after the service. Maybe a stolen glance or a smile or a wink, if we were very, very careful. It was just a way of showing the flag, as it were. In yo face, Girlfriend's-Mom! Elsewhere, our kisses were stolen, and honey-sweet, and I dreamed of someday loving my little blonde angel with all the hot, vague passion of adolescent ingenuousness. When I came to graduate from high school and head off to the University, the blonde angel simply couldn't bear contemplating the woes and stress of the foreseeable future, with us separated by many unbridgeable miles and many doleful circumstances, not to mention the unrelenting opprobrium of her mother. I got formally and ritually dumped -- hard. First time dumped, zero mental preparation. The pain of that loss nearly yanked the carpet from under my final grades, and here I was hoping to go out of high school in a blaze of academic glory. In retrospect, it was simply an act of survival on her part. Neither of us had the savoir-faire to talk out the issues and develop any sort of contingency plan. We would have only needed to deal with two years' forbearance, but we lacked the perspective to see the picture that way. Or maybe it was only me who lacked. Farewell, little blonde angel.

I moped my way through a summer job that should have been three months in Paradise for a seventeen-year-old young man. I'd been taken on as a handy-boy at a <u>Girl Scout Camp</u>! Two hundred girls! Of course, nearly all of those girls were eleven and twelve years old. Scared to death of the only male in camp (excepting the 83-year-old caretaker, who, naturally, didn't count). But then after a couple weeks, at least a hundred and fifty of all those little girls had gotten over their timidity and developed passionate secret crushes on Yrs Trly, the only male in camp. I'd drive about on the dusty forest lanes in my rattletrap, topless jeep, going about my doings, and lines of little girls along the roadside would wave and simper and shout Hi and try to get me to say Hi back, and dissolve into embarrassed giggle-fits whenever I did. Well, of course then there were the counselors. Lovely, self-confident college sophomores and juniors, for the most part. Treated me like a little brother. Perfectly cordial, nice even…but who among them was interested in any form of social, not to mention *romantic*, liaison with a fresh-out-of-high-school seventeen-year-old? My fragile self-image suffered further, and I spent the summer mostly nursing the broken heart left me back in June by my little blonde angel.

Does all this sound mockingly jejune? Pathetic? Puerile? Puppyish and poignant? Well…maybe so, maybe so. But the emotions were genuine, and a person should have a little empathy for the young, and not act so jaded and above-it-all. The young are

5

trying to learn hard lessons, and it doesn't always go so well. There really isn't any instruction book.

On the day I went off to the University, I experienced the sort of born-again epiphany like the one that all those hardcore Evangelical Christians speak of. Do you remember *The Wizard of Oz*? The 1939 movie, with Judy Garland? Of course you do – who doesn't? You'll recall that the first ten or fifteen minutes is filmed in high-contrast black-and-white, with maybe a bit of sepia toning thrown in. Then Dorothy gets conked on the head by a windowscreen and her farmhouse goes whirling up in the tornado's funnel. It tumbles down and goes crash, right in the shrubbery of Munchkin-Land. Dorothy creeps to the door and pushes it open. Through the door lies Oz, and everything from then on is in Technicolor. That was what happened to me on that first day at the University: I went through a door and the whole world became Technicolor.

At last, in an instant, in the wink of an eye, I was independent – entirely on my own! I had a room in a dorm, and a roommate, and twenty floormates to get to know. They were all incredibly smart! And many of them from interesting, faraway places! They manifested exciting intellectual hungers that had prodded them to gain admission into this particular University. There was more! I would never have to share living-space with my domineering older brother ever again in life! And there was an entire dormitory housing three hundred college girls, nearly all of them freshmen, bright-green with innocence just like me, standing no more than fifty yards north of my dorm room's picture window. All those college girls shared a dining-hall with us guys! And social mixers! Cookouts! Dances and parties! TV rooms and gamerooms and lounges, oh my! I was enrolled in a university ranked among the top ten institutions of higher learning in the country…top twenty in the entire world! The entire GALAXY, as far as anyone knew. Nearly thirty thousand students. Eleven hundred faculty. Twenty-seven Nobel Laureates on-staff in that mellow autumn of 1964. A short while into my tenure there, Ronald Reagan was pandering to the conservative masses in an attempt to get elected Governor. Ronnie was to aver that, at our particular school, all any of us radical student-types were majoring in was Sex, Drugs, or Treason! Not true, exactly, but my oh my did we enjoy that characterization. I was told by the Associate Dean himself, on my second day on-campus, that I could take fifteen units of credit – five full-time courses – every semester plus summer term for *three hundred years* before exhausting the catalog of undergraduate curriculum. That campus and its encapsulating college town was alive with culture, music, art, multifarious ethnicities, social ferment, intense politics, weirdness, debate, protest, streetcorner rarees, buskers, wacked-out urban wanderers, poets and writers, boulevard watercolorists, fortunetellers, dimly-lit shops, fragrant eateries, pushcarts, hawkers, rampant intellectualism…and a whole lotta very pretty girls! Even the less-than-very-pretty ones were cute and lively and bright! Morning and evening, a campus tower's mellow carillon rang out a free concert of slow, sweet melodies for half an hour. It was all *Technicolor*, and I was awash in it, abubble in it, <u>part</u> of it! Practically in a day, I stopped being a kid and leapt joyfully into adulthood. *Now*, I told myself, *if only I can find myself a nice girlfriend. And maybe, with her kind assistance, get laid.*

And in time, that came to pass. First, though, I had to learn a lot of stuff. I learned that, as Josh Billings once said (and every ensuing American folk-philosopher re-quoted as if it were an original thought), it's not what a man don't know that makes him a fool…it's what he knows that *ain't so*. I was pretty well-educated for a brand-new freshman, but an awful lot of it *warn't so*. I learned that what you saw on the TV news every evening was a *story*, not the *news*. I learned that there are a hundred ways of looking at the simplest social issues, so a person ought to look -- particularly at other people's strident opinions -- with an eye keenly-honed by skepticism. I learned that there were fundamental choices in life that I had not already made, and here's me, seventeen years old, thinking I'd done all of that already. Take drugs, for instance. In fact, that's the model I witnessed left, right and center, almost from my first hour at the University: "Take drugs!" Grass figuratively grew at one's feet, and I'm not talking

7

about lawns. Acid metaphorically dripped, cheaply and availably, from clandestine taps. Heavier psychotropics were to be had, and without great difficulty. Horse. Speed. Mescaline. Coke. Mushrooms. Downers. Uppers. Well, I was either a total innocent or a freak-of-nature, considering the path I chose. I recall making the conscious decision that I was going to opt out of the Sixties Drug Scene. Nothing stuffed in my pipe and smoked, nothing down my gullet, nothing needled into my veins. No thank you, not my style, not for me. Wasn't always easy, but I managed. In later years, people, hearing my abjuration, said "Of <u>course</u> you took drugs! You were in college in the 'Sixties!!!'" I suppose they just put me down as a liar when I said I did not, but I did not. Ever. At all. A conscious decision, a fundamental choice. I swear to you I never beat my breast and preached to anyone about it – it's just the choice I made for myself and I tried to keep pretty-much quiet about it. Eventually I found <u>Patterns of Culture</u>, and Ruth Benedict explained I was probably Apollonian rather than Dionysian in my outlook. Okay, you probably have to read the book to know what all that means…or at least Google it up. That gentle explanation helped me a lot, along the road to understanding myself. A little bit later in life, in a faraway Southeast Asian country whose name you can probably guess (rhymes with "See it, Sam!"), the availability of pills and powders and herbal cigarettes was even more universal, and dirt-cheap, and the temptations, rationales, and peer-pressure were very much stronger…but I stuck to my resolve even then. I swear it!

And there's another thing I learned, something that in my naivete I had had no idea about, prior to an afternoon in May 1965…the springtime of my freshman year. There existed a faraway place in the world that was eventually to exert profound influence on my life, and its name was Viet Nam. Do you think you might want to *see it, Sam*?

And then there's all that stuff about girls that I learned. In my first September at the University, there was this one incredible little doll, so stylish and Big-City streetwise and well-liked that she actually had a *following*, seven or eight students, both sexes, who clustered around her like bees around a rose. Her operational *nom de guerre* was 'Candy', and how I longed to become the nougat filling in the scrumptious little bonbon of her adorable being. Well surprise! She took a liking to me. Waved me into an empty chair in an Anthropology lecture-hall one afternoon, a chair right up next to her sweet-smelling, sugar-coated little red-haired self that she'd rendered empty by the simple artifice of making one of her coterie get up and move. After that, we sat together during Anthropology lectures for the balance of the term. My attention lagged, insofar as Anthropology was concerned. It was Candy who orchestrated our first date. It was Candy who unbuttoned my first button, unzipped my first zipper, slid a warm, exciting hand into the first Yellow Zone I'd ever surrendered to any girl. It was Candy who guided my fingers, vibrating with anticipation, into the first feminine Red Zone those fingers ever knew the shape, texture and sweet, honey-scented moisture of. What Candy taught me was that *girls liked sex too*, and she was a really good teacher! Who knew?

Well, I was in-lust with Candy by the middle of my freshman year. I was spending an awful lot of lecture-time mooning over her instead of taking notes. I would flush and blush and breathe hard whenever I caught sight of her across the quad. At night I would drift into sleep having detailed fantasies about my yummy Chocolate Buttercream. I would wake up in the morning inexcuseably and embarrassingly erect, all for her sake alone, wishing desperately I would one morning magically wake up two inches away from her hot little cherry-lollipop body and actually get to *do* something about my pitiful aroused condition. And, oddly, being in-lust was gently metamorphosing to being in-love, as it became manifest to me that this girl was not a wicked, deceiving, immoral, sluttish freak of feminine nature, but a healthy, lusty young woman with a kind heart, generous moral principles, rampant sense of humor, and lively intellect whose feelings for me were on the up-and-up. For her long-term affections, I coulda been a <u>contender</u>! But naïve fool that I was, I failed to act with determination and dispatch. Another man, a grad-student, a mature man-of-the-world, tore her adamant interest away from me. She never promised to be exclusively *my* girl over the several months we dated, and I had neglected to ask her to.

9

She apologized sweetly for the pain she knew I was experiencing when she broke it off with me. That was the way the Candy crackled.

Then there was Love-Affair Number Two, and I must say I put what Candy had taught me to practical use. L.A.#2 was largely about untrammeled sex. And when I say sex, I don't mean capital-S Sex, because I was still far too timid and naïve for that level of intensity. But hoo-boy, just shy of it! The lucky recipient of my attentions in L.A.#2 (she begged me to call her 'Millie') was operating on a 24/7 sexual hair-trigger. I had to be careful when we danced close, because she'd go orgasmic standing-up if we rubbed a bit too much, and she inclined to be little *vocal*. I swear, she came in her undies one time when all I was doing was nibbling on her earlobe a little bit! Adding onto Candy's teaching, Millie taught me that girls could not only *like* sex, they can have *frantically insatiable appetites* for sex. Who knew? All of that was plenty fun, but there would have been no stopping, short of mutual sexually-induced coma, if ever we'd started fiddling-open each other's buttons, Millie and me. Then I came down with a cold which turned into pneumonia, and I wound up *hors de combat* for about three weeks in the University sick-ward. When I re-entered the Land of the Living, Millie, desperate for certain attentions, had moved on. Drat!

So it went for my freshman and sophomore years at the University. Little romances, small gains in self-confidence *vis a vis* the feminine gender, minuscule advances in learning about what made women tick…to the extent that anyone of the Male Persuasion ever actually knows. There weren't any courses in the topic on the undergraduate curriculum. I had to find out everything for myself, experimentally. So I had some sweet times. Had some scary relationships, like Luz, a girl who was so outrageously fertile that I was reluctant to kiss her too hard – she'd have gone immaculately hyperpregnant in an instant, and she had a lot of scary-looking older brothers and uncles who were already eying me balefully, who would have turned violent if that lovey little gumdrop had come up preggers. Luz was of indigenous Northern-Mexican ancestry. Yaqui. Before European contact, the Navajo were a pretty fearless bunch, but they lived in dread of one other neighboring warrior-race: the various bands of Apache. The Apache were just plain mean, don't-mess-with-us SOB's. Rattlesnakes and Grizzly-bears got out of their way, and the Apache weren't afraid of *anybody or anything*. ...Except the Yaqui. Such secretive, sneaky-eyed, fiercely-private wildland assassins that neither the Conquistadores nor any subsequent would-be oppressor ever managed to completely subdue the Yaqui, and they are the only North American indigenous people who have continuously maintained some form of self-governance since the time of Columbus. As for me, I wasn't actually *afraid* of that lovey little Yaqui gumdrop – in fact, I rather liked Luz...but her brothers and uncles were another matter. Well during those first couple of college years I even had one on-again-off-again girlfriend who was...a *friend*. I could call Karen up without agenda or preamble and put together an impromptu social event without any sort of mating-dance. She felt at liberty to call *me* up, and did with great frequency...in fact, she seemed to have radar that would tell her when I was a little down, and the phone would ring, and it would be her, all cheery and lovey. I could talk with Karen about anything, and I do mean anything. She gave me quirky little gifts and sent me hand-painted cards for no reason whatsoever, and I sincerely hope I remembered to reciprocate. Physically, we could venture onto exciting yet scary ground, regarding sex and ecstasy, without having to get all apologetic or committed...for no more profound reason than giving each other pleasure and comfort. I loved Karen well enough, and think of her fondly to this day. But the friendship never progressed to the next level. More's the pity...in retrospect years later, I realized that she and I never had a single cross word in over three years off-and-on dating, and we smiled and laughed all the time. Maybe she and I should have serioused-up about each other.

Well, then, all this time I was learning other things as well. Perhaps my grades weren't *cum laude*, which we can of course put down to the abovementioned distractions, but I was sticking in there, in no grave danger of suffering grade-point collapse. One semester I took it in my head to take a five-unit class in

Introductory Spoken Russian! What was I <u>thinking</u>? Self-flagellation for imaginary sins? Brazenly tempting the wild Demons of Flunking-Out? What motivated me was my having bought a recording of highlights from Modest Mussorgsky's opera, <u>Boris Godunov</u>. Just loved those baritone and basso-profundo arias! Tried to sing along! Needed desperately to know what those fools were bellowing about! So for no better reason than that, I enrolled in Introductory Spoken Russian. *Bozhe moi*! *Nye ochen harascho*! Never worked so hard on a single course in my entire college career, for the reward of a squeaker C-minus! *Pravilnye*!

I bumbled along with a loosely-declared major in Biological Sciences. The buzzwords attached to this particular curriculum were "Ecological Field Studies". In 1965, I don't think there were a hundred people on the face of the planet who knew the precise meaning of that word "ecology." Then one day in the middle of my junior year I was making my way across-campus trying not to be late for some boring lecture or another, and the weather was trying to confound me. It was raining like a firehose. I ducked into a building in the nether corner of the campus, thinking I could shortcut a hundred yards or so within its nice dry interior corridors, and I discovered, whaddyaknow! That building was the SCHOOL OF FORESTRY! Who knew we had a School of Forestry at this particular University? The more I thought about Forestry, the more convinced I was that I'd been missing something that was custom-made for the likes of me! A discipline with an <u>actual career-path</u>! At the time, you see, I had not the vaguest notion of what I might be able to do in the real world with a bachelor's degree in Ecological Field Studies. Continue into graduate school, maybe? Pump gas? Flip burgers? Ah, but Forestry! A career with numerous agencies public and private which actually recruited certified graduates in this field of expertise. A career combining biology, management, applied quantitative science, and business acumen...but in the *outdoors!* In the mountainous, forestey, pine-scented, underdeveloped, scantly-populated, pristine, river-bisected and lake-studded regions of the country! I knew I'd made a mistake not stumbling across this before, but I knew how to rectify that mistake!

I set up a couple of meetings with the associate dean of the Forestry Department. I steeled my parents to the idea of a switch in major. I examined my planned course schedule for the ensuing three semesters and realigned it to the Forestry curriculum. Bummer! Any way you sliced it, an additional undergraduate year was going to be necessary. My parents, good sports and Deep Pockets both, backed me up. The associate dean lined up the paperwork for admission to the program. I was going to be IN! Oops…one little fly in the ointment, and that was my <u>Draft Board</u>, God bless 'em.

I had turned eighteen a short while before all that Viet Nam Day hoopla. I had docilely registered for the draft, like I was supposed to. They'd had the very first draft-number lottery, and my number was disappointingly low. A hundred nine or thereabouts. Not one of the first dozen, but nowhere near high enough to make it unlikely they'd get around to me. Not with the kind of Army ramping-up the LBJ Administration had in mind as the whole Viet Nam thing got hotter. So when I began to consider continuing my undergraduate education into a fifth year, due to the change in major, I wrote a nice letter and mailed it off to my Draft Board asking them if all this would be all right with them.

The reply was disappointing:

"Well harrumph harrumph normally we expect you to graduate in FOUR years to maintain a student deferment, young man. And you've got to maintain a full academic load! At least fifteen units a semester. A fifth year?…well, we don't know about that. We're going to have to just wait and see…."

This was not exactly a response I could take to the bank. Worse comes to worst, I figured I'd have ways to stall a little bit, like my right to formally appeal any draft-board finding and so forth. Maybe I'd make it through that fifth year…maybe. I went ahead and put in the paperwork for the change of major.

Along about this time I landed another summer-job at a camp.

Only, instead of lowly handyboy for the Girl Scouts, this was a full-fledged counselor position at a rich-kid's expensive private camp up in the mountains. A co-ed camp, which meant co-ed staff! And I was nearly nineteen, old enough to be on an equal footing with those *girl* counselors! The summer turned out blissful. The camp was clean and well-maintained, up in the aromatic pine-forests. It sat on a nice lake. I got the detail as the sailing instructor, and had charge of a tentful of "chipmunks"-- eight-year-old boys who hero-worshipped me as if I were a young God, on-loan from Olympus for the summer. I had driven my motorcycle up to the mountains figuring it would serve nicely as transportation on days off – my sweet, sleek Triumph made a major splash and was quite the reputation-booster. That summer, the Beach Boys were hugely popular, and the Staff Retreat had every surfin' hit they had ever recorded. About halfway through the summer, something went zing between me and a very hot young counselor-lady who ran the craft shop, and my life changed.

3
Someone Special for Me

Elle was amazing. Blonde, bright, busty, blue-eyed, pretty, self-confident. There wasn't a counselor on the "boy's" side of the Sacred Dividing Line who wouldn't have sacrificed his left arm at the elbow for a shot at her. But Elle had a way of knowing what she wanted when she saw it, and then going right after it. And it transpired that she wanted ME! Here's what happened.

There was always a nice afternoon breeze to sail by on the lake. But promptly at 4:00 p.m. every single day, the breeze died with the faintest final gasp like an elderly swan, and the lake became a windless mirror until the following morning. Knowing this, I scheduled afternoon sailing sessions to end at 3:30, so the kids could get the boats back to shore, chained-up for the night, all the tack and equipment back in the locker. One afternoon shortly after 3 o'clock I spotted Elle and another counselor-girl sailing out of our cove and off around the point, heading south downlake in one of my teeny little sailboats. A mile south was a little anchorage and a general store called MacDougal's. They had a snack bar that offered very nice ice-cream sundaes. My guess was that those two counselor-girls were hungry for ice-cream, and they'd swiped one of my sailboats to go fulfill their fantasy. In about half an hour they were going to find themselves becalmed like a couple of Ancient Mariners. When the mess-hall dinner gong rang at 6 p.m. and the two of them were stuck out on the lake, windless, nowhere near their respective bereft tablefuls of camper-girls, there was going to be Big Trouble and someone was going to get fired. More likely, TWO someones. So, I got the rest of the boats put away, locked up the gear and lifejackets, shooed the campers on up the trail to camp under the watchful eye of my assistant, and set out on a rescue mission.

I had a nice kayak as a supplement to my sailboat fleet. Very agile, very speedy. I paddled down the lake toward MacDougal's. I arrived at the anchorage to spot Elle and her companion rowing the sailboat around and around in erratic circles in the harbor, with lank, empty sails flapping against the mast. They'd pulled the centerboard out of its slot and detached the rudder to use as paddles. It wasn't going well at all, and it helped very little that they were both convulsed with laughter. Incriminating chocolate fudge-sauce was still visible, smeared on their lips.

"Throw me the painter," I hollered.

"The *what*?"

"That little rope thing with a loop in it at the bow...that's the *pointy* end of the boat." That accomplished, I tied it off onto a cleat on my trusty kayak and proceeded to tow them ignominiously back to camp. I'm pretty certain this towering, selfless, heroic deed was the instigator of Elle's fancy for me.

We started hanging out in the Staff Retreat after Taps. Then we started going on moonlight walks along the lakeshore. Ahhh...the First Kiss! Is there anything sweeter? Then we discovered that if we took a moonlight walk up toward the horse corral, rather removed from camp proper, there was a big stack of hay bales up there, with a few saddle-pads strewn about on top. We discovered that if we climbed up on top of that pile of hay bales, we could get real comfortable. And it was real private. We swiftly indulged in the Second Kiss. After that, we pretty-much lost count. We discovered that buttons and snaps and zippers and bra-hooks could be undone in reliable seclusion, up there on top of the haystack. Our moonlight makeouts started stretching until midnight, or one a.m., or maybe later. Sleep deprivation set in, but we were young and resilient. And late one night right before the end of the summer, Elle wangled out of me the appalling admission that, at age nineteen, I was still what you'd have to call virginal as regards er, um, actual sexual intercourse, so to speak. In a trice she wiggled out of the rest of her clothes and took care of that little detail on the spot, right up there on top of those fragrant bales of horse-hay. Something above half a quart of seminal fluid transferred custodianship, along with several million of my finest spermatozoa, eager volunteers one and all, God bless 'em.

Well, was that ever a Great Leap Forward in my education! There was less than a week left of camp for us to bang each other senseless after Taps every night, but we tried our best. Then the Last Day arrived. Campers onto the buses. Camp snugged down for the winter. Big Farewell Staff luncheon. There was a tearful parting, an exchange of phone-numbers, a flurry of vague promises. Back home, Elle attended college a long, long hundred miles away from me, and during the summertime there had been nebulous talk about a boyfriend back on her campus, and in point of fact I myself had been dating someone named Sally kind of exclusively toward the end of the spring semester, but without any what you could call binding promises made, so I'd steeled myself for the Elle thing turning out to have been just one of those summer affairs...not that I'd ever been favored by one of those summer affairs before. I strapped my stuff onto my faithful Triumph, kicked her into growling life, and waved farewell as I sped away.

A small aside may be in order. As I review the first pages I've written, it seems as if I have laid bare more of my early romantic and sexual adventures than some readers might find comfortable to contemplate. But in truth, I believe that almost every young man who is normal and healthy in the libido department makes his way through similar discoveries. If you were counting, you would have to conclude that my amorous escapades were hardly over-plentiful. What I find as noteworthy in looking back on my early experiences is that I would have never made any progress against my own natural proclivity toward shyness and introversion, had it not been for the several healthy, lusty, self-assured young women, each of which had a certain tendency toward initiative in matters sexual, who took me out of my timidity and gave me such fulfillment as I experienced. I never tried to maintain multiple simultaneous lovers, I never felt like I was misusing any one of my lovers like a callous rogue. I loved them as well as I could, all in their turn. It was they who predisposed me to what came later in my life. Forgive me, if you can, for dealing so personally with my youthful *affaires de coeur* – the purpose of all that in this narrative is other than idle boastfulness.

Well, a week or so after the close of summer camp, back to the University I made my way. Autumn enrollment proceeded. We corresponded often, Elle and I. That was nice. She always splashed her letters with perfume. A time or two, we talked on the phone. Sally, it turned out, had sniffed out another boyfriend over the summer and as autumn semester commenced, she broke off whatever might have remained of our relationship by the simple, heartless expedient of refusing to speak so much as another syllable to me until I got the picture...so *that* little complication was off-the-table. Elle and I spoke vaguely about some kind of get-together, but there was a certain amount of bobbing and weaving from her end, so I did not press the issue. Then our House promulgated plans for a fall-semester Formal, to be held in November at a spiffy hotel in the City.

I asked Elle if she'd like to attend the Formal with me, in a nice letter...jotted into a sappy Hallmark card, as I recall. She evaded a direct answer with one of those I'll-have-to-get-back-to-you responses. I let some time go by. I let *a lot* of time go by. Then with only three weeks left until the Formal, I just had to have an answer. I phoned her up. We engaged in small talk, then I got around to the Formal. "Ohhh, sweetie," she sighed. "I just *can't*! I'm so sorry!"

"What's the trouble?" I asked her.

Turns out, it was that nebulous boyfriend thing. Turns out, he wasn't so nebulous after all. He and Elle had been steadies for a couple of years. Honesty being the best policy when there's no avoiding it, Elle had mentioned to him that she'd been invited to a Formal affair down in the City by a very nice boy she'd met at summer camp, and she was soliciting the boyfriend's okay to accept the invitation. Well, nebulous boyfriend had gone nuclear on her. A screaming row ensued. She'd been forbidden to even consider accepting my invitation, and had had insulting epithets hurled in her direction. Turns out, he was the possessive type, and a bit controlling to boot. Vulgar under pressure. Insanely macho. "He won't let me go. Can you forgive me?" Elle begged.

I considered my response for a few seconds, then replied. "Elle...it's obviously your decision to make...not mine, and probably not your boyfriend's either, if you think about it. I won't tell you I'm not disappointed, because I was really looking forward to seeing you again. But if you can't do it, you can't. It's not going to affect our friendship, I hope. I can still write to you, okay?" Very much chastened by this turn of events, we exchanged a few vague kindnesses and rang off.

Imagine my surprise when two days later Elle phoned me back. "Did you invite someone else to that Formal yet?" she asked.

"There IS no one else, Elle."

"Can I accept then?"

I agreed, overjoyed. "What made you change your mind?" I had to ask.

She explained it all. Here was this one guy she'd been dating hot-and-heavy for a couple years, all the way back to high school, who by mutual arrangement she'd put on-hold for the summer, as he had her. In fact, cooling-it for the summer had been *his* suggestion, and under a bit of pressure he had admitted to a serial string of summertime dalliances, full-up sexual bang-fests fueled by alcohol and pot, but "absolutely nothing serious – just messing around," in his own words. At least two of the recipients of his non-serious attentions were pestering him daily with passionate importuning as the summer faded to autumn, Elle entirely notwithstanding. In the matter of my invitation, he'd treated Elle like shit, screamed authoritarian demands at her, called her slutty names. Then here was this other guy she hadn't known very long, to whom she had no particular obligations, who'd been supportive and understanding, kept his cool, told her gently that it was her decision to make, bared his feelings about his affection for her, and his feelings of disappointment in the turndown. And in spite of everything, wanted to stay friends. Which one was the Schmuck and which one was the Treasure? She had explained these relational revelations of hers to the Schmuck, had returned his Class Ring and his letter-sweater and a couple of stuffed bears he'd given her for her birthday, gratuitously slit-open across their little plush bellies with a pair of eyebrow scissors, and had broken it off severely with the jerk-face asshole. From then on, I was her Treasure. And I worked pretty hard to try to deserve it. And yes, we had a lovely time at the Formal Affair, and at one-thirty a.m. sneaked off to a little apartment a good friend of mine had vacated for the night, occupied the first genuine bed we had yet known together, and made naked sweat-drippy love for hours and hours like crazed monkeys in heat.

We got along so well...so well! Cumulatively we drove thousands of miles, both of us alternately, to spend weekends together. Got ardently into skiing together, up in the mountains. And camping-out under the stars in fine weather. Sailing on the bay. And walks along the beach. Picnics in the park. Went to the movies. Wrote impassioned letters to each other when we should have been studying, back at our respective colleges. When we were together, we made love every chance we got, every way we could figure out how. I got more proficient in my college studies, through the simple expedient of not having to waste energy gawping at any of the co-eds anymore. Elle was in my life and I was content with her, only her.

Eventually, she invited me to come visit her at home and meet her parents. That was a big step. But, turned out *they liked me*! During that weekend we even managed to go off to the movies one night, just the two of us, and then on the way home we parked the car in a deserted cul-de-sac in an under-construction subdivision Elle knew about, and screwed each other crazy for an hour or so in the cramped front-seat of the car. It was the first time she had primal-scream fist-banging serial orgasms, and I don't mind confessing it was a little startling, seeing her go wacko like that. On reflection, I felt a peculiar satisfaction in having taken her to that place. Pretty certain *she* felt a particular satisfaction as well. For the rest of it though, we minded our manners for the balance of that weekend.

And then I invited her to come spend a weekend with me, meet *my* folks and siblings and near-relations at the Family Compound back in my home-town. Our residential establishment was reminiscent of the Kennedy Family Compound in Kennebunkport, I'm sure, although I've never yet been a guest of the Kennedys. It was a big sprawly suburban lot with plenty of trees, miscellaneous outbuildings, a massive firepit suitable for barbecuing anything from hot dogs up to a spitted Cape Buffalo, and a long rambling ranch-house that had been built in the early 1950's by my Uncle Jimmy. That house, the odd domicile I'd grown up in, was at heart a complex, totally unique do-it-yourself project. My family, it transpires, was a hotbed of do-it-yourselfism going back many generations. My mother's brother James was a self-taught carpenter who believed in building 'way beyond code, just in case of 250-mph gales or 40-foot snowloads or stray tsunamis or earthquakes reading in at 11.5 on the Richter Scale. Never use a 16-penny nail when you can use a 24-penny, was Uncle Jimmy's credo. Two-by-twelves are better than two-by-eights in all circumstances. That house would have remained smugly, defiantly intact after a near-miss thermonuclear airburst. The rest of the Family Compound was unalloyed quirkiness in all respects, all adobe walls and masonry patios and redwood trellises and overgrown vegetation, set-about with doghouses and greenhouses and toolhouses and an honest-to-goodness bronze statuary foundry out under the redwood trees. My father, in his retirement, as it came about, had eschewed the engineering mindset, taken up sculpture, and ever afterward derived artistic inspiration from the late Auguste Rodin. In the backyard foundry, he sought to create massive bronze sculptures of muscular, nude women and truncated, twisted torsos of muscle-rippling men with unapologetic outward-thrusting genitalia. I apprenticed for him once – gloved, helmeted, dressed in head-to-toe silvery nomex suits, the two of us had furnace-melted and poured 280 pounds of reeking liquid bronze into two separate red-glowing plaster molds fresh from the burnout kiln, with great success. A female torso with spectacular nipply breasts, and the portrait bust of a notorious Seventeenth-Century Caribbean pirate by the name of Red-Legs Greaves, who ostensibly was a direct lineal ancestor of both us artisans. Red-Legs sits in gruff defiance on a bookshelf in my dining-room, to this very day, all green with verdigris. So anyway, I was filled with anxiety as to how Elle would take this eclectic mélange that was my childhood home. And, worse yet was the inescapable fact that the Family Compound was inhabited by *my parents*. AND, *my brothers*! Challenging personalities, every one. I need not have worried…she adored it all, the whole mess…and everyone <u>loved</u> her, right on down to the dogs and cats. *Yeah… I thought, for perhaps the first time. …So do I!*

We didn't get in a big rush about it, though. Six or seven months later, one of Elle's longtime girlfriends got married. We were invited to the wedding. It was just the sort of affair the human race has seen about thirty billion times since the beginning of recorded history. Laughter and tears. White satin gowns. Dark suits for the men, with colorful neckties. Flowers and ribbons and strings of lights. Children running amok. A line of bridesmaids cute as a parcel of ladybugs. Insouciant ushers in cummerbunds. Wine and cake and iced fruit punch and miscellaneous nibblies. Sweet, somber, sappy music. Age-old ritual. A staid, cassocked functionary clutching a Bible. Sacred words and ardent promises. The affirming kiss, the joyful promenade. Toasts, embarrassing anecdotes. Dancing. More laughter, more tears. Piles of gifts and flower bouquets. Elle and I held hands a lot, and never left each other's side. She introduced me as 'her special friend', and I wondered where that designation might be leading. There were covert, speculative glances passed between us. I admit to having been the speculative glancer, more than once. At the reception, little bags of rice had been furnished for throwing upon the Wedding Couple's eventual departure, each one a gauzy white mesh fabric pouch secured with a satin ribbon threaded through a cheap, glitzy little plastic-replica engagement ring. Elle facetiously slipped the ring from her rice-bag and pushed it onto my finger, punctuating it with a nice kiss with some surreptitious champagne-flavored tongue in it that held the promise of quite a little bit more later, when she got me alone and could wiggle out of her very festive, very sexy satin cocktail dress. So I reciprocated…I unribboned *my* rice-bag and bedecked *her* finger with its silvered plastic ring.

Both of us had chosen the appropriate digits: ring-finger, left hand. It was all in fun, a spontaneous act of zany flirtatiousness. But Elle wore that crummy, cheap little ring I'd given her for the next year and a half, never taking it off. As for wearing the cheap crummy ring she'd given me...so did I. For the next year and a half. I still have it somewhere. It's down in the bottom of my sock drawer, I believe.

She kept wearing that plastic gimcrack until the warm, moonlit night I gave her a better one...gold, with a small but immaculate, exquisite diamond. Without a moment's hesitation she said Yes to the earnest question that went with the ring.

4

My Life Takes a Few Fortuitous Turns

We were married in June. Originally, we had planned it would be the June we both graduated from college. But I had that extra-year thing which went along with the switch in major. Elle had taken a lighter course-load for a few terms, because she was working part-time in order to pay her college expenses and living costs. It meant that she would not be graduating in June either. Rather than put off marriage for another year, we resolved to go ahead on the original schedule and to become a pair of struggling, starving married students. The folklore was filled with examples of how this kind of suffering made for strong marital relationships. So, in June of 1968, we married.

We scraped up the funds for a modest wedding. There were about twenty guests. A simple banquet afterwards. We booked a small Congregational Church that had no air-conditioning. During the brief service, it was 114 degrees Fahrenheit in the church, and Elle almost cracked up suppressing giggles at the drops of sweat dripping off the Reverend's nose and splashing on the Holy Bible. Later, she asked me if I thought that runoff might have diluted the efficacy of the vows it was dampening. I didn't imagine so.

We honeymooned in one of North America's most beautiful National Parks. My parents staked us to a suite for three nights in the grand old hotel that had reigned over that park for a hundred years or more, and the staff treated us like honeymooning royalty. My dad let us take his bright-red Porsche on that little trip.

When we came home, we packed up our meager belongings in Elle's beatup Comet and drove upstate. I had a summer job with the State Division of Forestry. We settled in to married existence of the most frugal kind imaginable. It was unalloyed bliss

At the end of the summer, we came back down to civilization, re-enrolled in our respective colleges. Elle had transferred to a different state-college campus that was only about fifteen miles from the University, and she had only a single term left to complete. I had another full academic year. It was going to be tight going, financially. But we were young and naïve and thought we could handle it.

Then I started getting letters from that pesky Draft Board, God bless 'em.

At first they wanted me to drop everything and come take a pre-induction physical. There was a preliminary medical checklist for me to fill out, which included this question:

Are you taking any prescription medications at present?

Well heck yes! Toward the end of the summer, I'd taken a nasty fall out in the woods and scraped all the skin off of one shin. It had gotten a bit infected. The University health clinic had put me on some kind of antibiotic. A *prescription* antibiotic.

Imagine my delight when it took my Draft Board four months to chew on that fact! I didn't get another testy missive until about half-past-January.

While my Draft Board was chewing, a stratagem occurred to me. I would go into the Navy enlistment office and see if I could make application for Naval Officer-Candidate School. My hypothesis was that as a junior-grade Naval officer, I'd probably be better off than an enlisted grunt toting an M16 out in some Vietnamese rice paddy. AND, it was likely to take months and months to run me through an extensive battery of tests, medical exams, background checks and whatnot. Meanwhile, I'd be able to finish my degree program. Now, I was not so sanguine as to imagine that the United States Navy was lusting for BS graduates in *Forestry* to bolster its officer corps, but it seemed pretty likely that this tactic would buy me enough time to get finished with college. I'd probably get turned down by the Navy, and wind up an M16-toting grunt after all, but I was careful not to tell Elle this. Elle thought the OCS strategem was quite wily, as she was dead-set against imagining me slogging through any stinkin' Vietnamese rice paddies. Also I think maybe, in her febrile little imagination, she was picturing how dashing I'd look in an Ensign's dress-Whites.

Well, I was mistaken in my estimate of how much time the Navy OCS application would buy me. Instead of four or five months' forbearance, I didn't hear a squeak from my Draft Board for almost two years! God bless 'em!

5

I Break Into the Working World and Come Close to Being Blown Up with Dynamite

I finished my Bachelor's program at last. Five years at the University was about all I had the stomach for. I desperately wanted into the workforce. It was only a matter of time before I wound up in the military – my Draft Board had made that clear – so any job I found would be a temporary hiatus. Unfortunately, every prospective employer in the Western Hemisphere understood that fact as well. Over the spring I sent out three dozen inquiries stapled to three dozen resumes. I got back three-dozen-minus-one turndowns. I got back one grudging letter from a logging/milling company in Oregon, grumblingly stating that I could have a menial, low-paying job in the logging-woods if I really wanted one. Setting chokers.

Now, a freshly-falled tree, cut up into logs, is a big heavy ungainly thing, usually lying perched uneasily on a steep slope. A 'choker' is a long, heavy, kinky, rusty length of wire-rope (what the uninformed would probably call "cable") that must be somehow wrapped around an eleven-ton log lying smack-down against the ground. The choker is then "buttoned", i.e. hooked into a sliding noose ("choker"…get it?) through a big heavy chunk of iron called the "choker bell" that rides along the rope. You then hook the spliced eye on the far end of the choker onto a gigantic bulldozer or a wildly-thrashing high-lead logging system, then run like hell through the briars and the brambles in order to avoid being crushed to paste when the log starts moving. Repeat every two minutes, all day long. Unsafe, backbreaking, filthy, monotonous, ill-paid work at the bottom of the logging-woods employment totem pole.

I took the job.

Once again, Elle and I packed our meager belongings into her sad, tired Comet. We headed for Oregon. On arriving, we found a tiny house to rent. The security deposit virtually exhausted our cash supply. On Monday I started to work – at 3:45 a.m.

My on-the-job training consisted of a very grouchy logging-boss saying, "This is a choker. There are some logs. Get to work, Goddammit!" By the time that first day was over, I was five times dirtier than on the worst day of my life so far. I was dragging, I was starving. But I was still alive. I consoled myself by saying that it probably beat packing an M16 in a Vietnamese rice paddy since nobody was actually *shooting* at me, and that I was learning about the commercial aspects of forestry from the ground up. I got home to find that Elle had spent her day rendering our spare little rental-house into a sweet, lovely home for us, a retreat, a lovenest set about with the adorable flowery touches of her personality. Then in the afternoon, she'd gone out and drummed up a job. Dressing windows in the local department-store, at minimum wage. A dollar seventy-five an hour, back in those days. Fringe benefits? Are you *kidding?*

The logging operations were routinely thirty or forty miles from town. We'd have to show up, rain or shine, at the headquarters compound before 4 a.m., jump into a filthy rustbucket pickup-truck aptly called a "crummy" in logger's parlance, and drive one or two hours to the job. No pay for those hours in transit, going or coming home. I swiftly discovered that loggers were some of the most colorful speakers of English I'd met in my sheltered life. Colorful, in the most obscene sense of the word.

"Look at that fuckin' cocksucker!" I'd hear, and discover that my attention was being directed toward a beautiful Cascade Lily growing along the roadside. Now, I'd have been happy to just fit in with the guys, but I lacked spontaneous fluency with the vocabulary. Moreover, it didn't seem wise to wave about the knowledge that I'd just graduated from a prestigious university with a degree in Forestry, when most of my compatriots had been lucky to have graduated from the third grade. I kept my B.S. under my hat. My protective steel hardhat. Also, I entertained fears that my given name was maybe a little formal, or perhaps insufficiently manly for a set that went by monikers like "Red" and "Dutch" and "Killer" and "Sly." I introduced myself using a nickname my dad had often used, derived from the first syllable of the family name. The nickname took root and blossomed.

About a month into my adventures as a logger, the five-person crew I worked with was pulled away to handle a special duty. A primitive road was being pioneered down a mountainside to access a remote stand of timber ripe for harvest. We were detailed to blow stumps.

Along the right-of-way for this road, trees ranging up to six feet in diameter had been falled, bucked into logs, and dragged away. Ah, but the *stumps*! Too big to grub out of the ground with the big D-8 Caterpillar that 'Red', our beer-gutted catskinner, operated. Very much in the way for the next step in roadbuilding. We had to laboriously drive a hole down under each stump's roots with a demon-invented, torturous hand-tool called (as one might expect!) a Bull-Prick. Imagine a six-pound sliding hammerhead on a five-foot-long steel…wellll…bull prick. This was brutish, palm-blistering labor, so the least senior member of the team got the detail. That would be me. Once this little opening was driven, resulting in a two-inch diameter tube in the dirt called a "snake-hole", a one-pound stick of dynamite was thrust down to the bottom, using a handy tree-branch as a pusher. Did I mention that the dynamite stick had been prepped with a blasting cap? A less-than-stable, anything-could-set-it-off blasting cap? One backfilled the loaded snake-hole with dirt, backed off about ten feet, touched the cap's leadwires to a six-volt battery, averted one's eyes and covered one's ears. Not in that order.

Ka-BAM! The snake-hole was "sprung". Now you could pack about SEVENTY one-pound sticks of dynamite into the resulting cavity under that stump. One or two of them prepped with blasting caps, of course. Hook the leads up to a really long wire. Back 'way the hell off, and give it some spark. BLOWWIE! That fuckin' cocksucker stump would go into orbit. Oh…except unless it happened to be a *hemlock* stump. Then the titanic explosion would only succeed in splitting it up into seven or eight chunks, still rooted into the ground, and an hour of cat-work with that big D-8 would be required to grub out the remains. One interesting little nuance: the really long wire mentioned above started out about four hundred feet long. Four hundred feet was a nice safe distance to be removed from seventy sticks of dynamite about to go up. BUT! Each explosion vaporized the closest-in ten feet of the really long wire. The Company was too cheap to buy us a new one very often. Do the arithmetic here. By the end of the week, we were not all that far away from the stump about to be blasted. Logger-machismo required that the entire crew huddle down together around the fellow with the blasting plunger, a nice tight cluster exactly the radius of an airborne tree stump. Made a guy a little nervous!

Nevertheless, blasting stumps was kind of fun, once I got over the terror. Did that for about a week and felt pretty manly! Each night after relating my day's doings, Elle would check me over for ghastly wounds, then retire to bed and weep herself to sleep.

In late July it clouded up and rained for a solid week. This was totally unexpected by Yrs Trly…summers were supposed to be hot and dry. But this was Oregon, remember. By the end of that week I was like a drowned rat, raingear notwithstanding. On Day Five of continual downpour, the grouchy logging-boss greeted me at 3:45 a.m. at the door of the crummy with "Yer laid off! Too fucking wet to log." It was made plain to me that I was NOT on salary, and therefore would not be receiving compensation for this -- or any other -- day of inclement weather. The specter of upcoming Winter breathed its icy exhalation down my neck: four or five months without pay. I went on home, wondering why he couldn't have grouched that message to me over the phone while going back to sleep might still have been an option.

By eleven o'clock that morning, I'd been staring out the kitchen window at unrelenting rainfall for quite a while. I'd drunk so much coffee I sloshed. This logging business certainly had its *downs*, I'd decided. Its *ups*…not so much. I should point out, I was being paid three dollars and five cents an hour, before taxes, for my labors. I struggled back into my raingear and hiked half a mile to the nearest US Forest Service Ranger Station. There, I begged an audience with whoever handled recruitment and hiring. A nice lady moped out from the back office and listened to my plea. Her facial expression was not encouraging. I identified myself to the nice lady as a recent University graduate in Forest Management, and all of a sudden the atmosphere got a lot more cordial. It occurred to me that this nice lady probably saw an uninterrupted stream of grubby laid-off loggers, lacking in the matter of education or credentials, hoping for the steady paycheck of a Gov'mint Job. I was given applications to fill out, the papers were forwarded to a higher-up office somewhere, and I was ushered out the door. Six weeks later, six weeks of continuous grueling labor at the business-end of a jaggedy choker, I got a letter from the USFS. Good news! We've got a job for you! That marked the end of my career in hands-on logging. Elle was even more relieved than I.

6

My Dream Job in the Forest

Thus began the next eleven years of my career-track with the Forest Service. With a couple years time-out for other life-altering pursuits, about which I'll tell you shortly.

We had to move, but not very far. The posting was to an idyllic Ranger District nestled in a lovely river-valley about fifty miles south of that grungy lumber-mill town. The District comprised half-a-million of the most beautiful forested acres on the planet. Streams, lakes, mountains range-on-range, crags and cliffs, deep brooding forests of tall conifers, a riot of wildflowers in every meadow, lava-fields, high wilderness terrain, snowcapped volcanic peaks, little cabins in the woods, no less than TWO ski areas operating on permit within National Forest boundaries, several summer camps operating under similar arrangement – Boy Scouts, Church-camp, Campfire Girls. Deer, bear, elk, eagles, badgers, lynx, raccoons. A zillion species of tweetie-birds. Bugs, lizards, snakes, frogs. Fish! Oh lord, the fish in those rivers and streams and lakes! I was in my element. Elle was in Paradise.

With a week of choker-setting to go prior to my big job-change, I suggested that Elle drive on down to our new posting to see what she could work out as to living arrangements. Before she departed, I suggested, "Try to find a place we can rent that has a little land attached. If we've got some pasture, maybe we can pick up a horse or two."

This was the Holy Grail for that girl. Since she'd been six years old, she'd been horse-insane. Her daddy had always promised her a horse, and the margins of her textbooks were still embellished with little sketches of the silky-maned Arab stallion she dreamed about. Due to the demands of a checkered career, and a move of household every year or two, her daddy had never been able to make good on the promise. Elle was not going to come back without having found us suitable quarters...us AND her hypothetical horse! I doubt she would have given up short of bloody murder with an axe, to get what we needed.

Elle, as usually the case, prevailed. She'd driven around the little village near my presumptive Ranger Station, just outside the National Forest boundaries, looking at sad, sagging rental quarters. She'd quizzed everyone she encountered, even stopping walkers along the country lanes to ask for rental possibilities. At last, she'd found her way to the middle-aged brother of a woman who lived a thousand miles away in California with her hubby and two kids. They had bought a two-story bungalow in this bucolic little community with the idea of moving north in a couple of years, when hubby reached retirement age. They were anxious to have a reliable young couple occupy the place so it wouldn't stand vacant.

What would prove to be our first real home was three bedrooms, two baths, living-room, country kitchen. It was all very rustic, fully furnished right down to food in the pantry and linens on the creaky brass bed. The house was all shingled-over with split cedar shakes -- roof and exterior walls. The house stood in a deep forest of conifers and rhododendrons, completely secluded, with five hundred feet of private frontage on a fine-looking river that positively churned with trout, pleading to be caught. By way of outbuildings, there was a disreputable lean-to garage affair we could park under. There was a pumphouse. There was a little storage-shed. There was a gigantic stack of firewood, for the place was heated by means of a huge fieldstone fireplace that had an insatiable appetite for wood. There was even a *Jeep* that went with the place! Ostensibly, the Jeep was part of the deal because this wonderful house was about a quarter-mile up a private stony lane which proved difficult when there was snow on the ground. Most important of all, this rustic ménage stood on *ten acres of fenced horsepasture*! The middle-aged brother thought that Elle and I would be just perfect as caretaker-tenants. The rent was $100 a month. Damn, Elle! *Well done*!

The week-end we moved, Elle had sleuthed-out one more thing: a pair of fat, sassy horses who had been put out to pasture a few years before when the little girls for whom they'd been originally bought grew out of their horse-crazy years and went boy-crazy instead. These horses had the run of 160 acres of graze – all in one huge enclosing fence. No cross-fencing, no corrals.

We were handed a pair of halters and told, "Go get 'em...they're yours for $50 apiece if you can catch 'em." Anticipating the chase of our lives, Elle and I waded out into waist-deep grass toward where the distant pair grazed, ears suddenly atwitch, on the *qui-vive* for approaching trouble. But instead of racing away like the wind, these two sweeties stood tranquilly, with only the slightest touch of equine curiosity on their long furry faces, while we sidled up and slipped the halters over their cooperative heads. Docile as puppies, the both of them, we led them back to the stock-trailer we'd rented, loaded them up, and drove them to the new home all of us would share. Elle was so afloat on a tide of bliss that she got on top of me and nearly screwed me comatose in gratitude that night, weeping for joy the entire time, and had there been any morsel of her heart she'd kept locked away from me in reserve, the elation of the gift of those silly horses would have earned me access. Exhausted by extremes of intercourse, she sighed in my ear as we drifted toward slumber, "The only thing that would have made it the teeniest bit better, Lover, is if you could manage to fuck me on *horseback!*" I cannot imagine how she'd have shown her daddy gratitude, if ever he'd been able to deliver on that horsey promise of his.

The line-back buckskin was a mare, plump as a beer-keg. Ink-black mane, tail and stockings. Big dark limpid eyes, tiny little muzzle...very suggestive of Arab blood in her ancestry. Faint dapples on her callipygian rump. She looked like one of those drawings on the cave wall at Lascaux or Altamira. She was in the prime of her life, fecund as only a healthy mare can be. The only time her gentle personality altered was when she was in-season, and then she manifested an implacable equine sluttiness that was comical to watch. In her delirium, she imagined that everything which moved – including dogs, automobiles, the larger specimens of avifauna, and Yrs Trly – might very possibly be the randy stallion she was longing for...and quite a few objects that *didn't* move, like haybales and rhododendron bushes for example. All and sundry were enthusiastically presented with her broad rump for immediate servicing, the tail alluringly cranked over to one side. The rangy pinto was, unfortunately for the buckskin mare, a gelding, with a droopy lower lip and a canny sense of where to put his feet. We named them Clytemnestra and Agamemnon. We shortened this up to Clyde and Aggie, because we soon found that the classical reference consistently went over the heads of the rustic element in our little mountain community. They all thought the new young forester and his pretty blonde bride were a little loopy, naming the mare "Clyde" and the gelding "Aggie". Perhaps they imagined our ability to tell the fundamental difference between boy and girl was somehow impaired. We never bothered to explain.

The ensuing fourteen months were the sweetest episode of serene bliss that two young people in love could ever imagine. I was working in my chosen field, hiking around out in the sublime forests and the fresh, crisp, conifer-scented mountain air nearly every day. Elle was blossoming in a setting she'd daydreamed about all her life, but never imagined she would actually inhabit. It was as if we'd ridden that rustic farmhouse up inside the tornado's funnel and then over the rainbow, and here we were, plumped down in the shrubbery someplace very like Munchkinland. To boot, I have had a bit more experience with saddle-horses since those long-ago days, but there was never a pair of more sweet-natured creatures than Clyde and Aggie. We rode nearly every day when the weather was nice, often bareback but sometimes using a pair of antique western saddles we'd borrowed from a neighbor. Both of them came without hesitation when called, like a pair of big goofy dogs, galumphing at the gallop, and submitted placidly to the saddle and bit.

We had the balance of a blissful summer in 1969, then a long, slow slide through Indian Summer into wintertime. I had never lived a winter in snow-country, and neither had Elle. We made the adjustment well enough. The first significant snowfall turned our little hollow into a crystal wonderland. Had the snow been green, it would have been very much like the Emerald City of Oz. It was only twenty-five miles to the nearer of those two ski-resorts, and we skied ourselves silly. Lift tickets were five bucks in 1969. Next there came a gentle spring bursting with wildflowers and does nursing fawns on our back lawn while bunny-rabbits frolicked in the greeny-grass, all festooned with gowans, and wild berries fattened on their stickery vines. Then an exciting summer, with my usual daily forestry work punctuated by the thrill and hard toil of firefighting as July thunderstorms peppered the high country with lightning strikes. Forest fires meant a welcome bit of extra money on the pay-stub, since we were all on-duty for sixteen-hour days, with overtime and hazard-pay thrown in. During this long, lazy blissful interlude, we'd been making it on a net monthly paycheck of only $315. It didn't matter – we thought we were in Heaven. We had young friends to cultivate, and campouts and barbecues. Lots and lots of fishing. We took that Jeep up roads you wouldn't have thought a mule could negotiate. Ah, it was all a nature-study lesson in amazement. Once in a while, though, Elle offered the opinion that this wondrous idyll just couldn't possibly last. Something surely was going to come along and screw it all up for us.

Sure enough, in September of 1970 I got a letter from my Draft Board. God bless 'em.

Greetings! Your friends and neighbors have selected you to drop whatever you are doing and submit to induction into the Armed Forces of the United States of America. Your sorry ass is gonna get shipped to Viet Nam!

7

My Sorry Ass is Drafted

Well, that was all she wrote for the blissful forest idyll. We parted sadly with Aggie and Clyde, sold cheap to a Forest Service colleague with preadolescent kids. We packed up such belongings as we could fit into the car. We took a lingering walk around our little mountain paradise. Then we drove away. I have never been back.

I found a trailer-house for Elle to rent. It was a bit seedy, up on cinderblocks, stuffed in back of a suburban farmhouse in a smallish city fifty miles downriver from my Ranger District. The District staffing officer had promised me that my job would be held open for me, courtesy of the same US Government that was about to train me up as a soldier-boy and ship me overseas. Elle promised she could find some kind of job to keep her afloat. We had penciled-out a budget based on the meager stipend the Army would afford my wife, and added in nearly all of my even more meager pay as a boot-private enlisted man. It was pretty slim. But emotionally, Elle held it together. Her daddy had been an Air Force officer – a career man – so she held a certain stiff-upper-lip tolerance for the vagaries of military life.

Neither of us were particularly hawkish. Neither of us particularly rabid anticommunists. Both of us had taken our education at colleges which were hotbeds of radical thinking, very outspoken against the war in Viet Nam. If I'd been able to choose, I would not have voluntarily chosen military service. Not in a million years. I was pretty peaceable, and I still am. There was nothing of the aggressive gung-ho hero about me, and there still isn't. But when my friends and colleagues first became aware that I was on the verge of getting drafted, their sage advice started trickling in.

"Move to Canada! Or Sweden!"

"Shoot a toe off! Or better yet: contract an infection! Gonorrhea's a good one!"

"Here's a number to call...you can join this 'church' and

they'll vouch for you being a pacifist and a Conscientous Objector."

"Commit some minor crime, like shoplifting. Get caught and they'll never take you then!"

I thought of my dad's generation. One of his brothers, a naval officer graduated from Annapolis...killed by a Japanese 5-inch naval projectile in the Battle of Savo Island. His remains rest in the Punchbowl Cemetery on the island of O'ahu. A second brother, graduate of West Point, who had gone ashore over Omaha Beach on June 6 and survived with only a few shrapnel wounds. My father, Army OTC, rapid advance to Captain, three years in the Persian Gulf in charge of putting together lend-lease convoys for the relief of Stalingrad, then for equipping the Red Army's westward push into Germany. His last brother, younger than him. Graduate of Air Force Officer Training. A jet-fighter pilot through the entire duration of the Korean Conflict. Shot down twice. Rescued both times. Metal plate in his skull from one of those misadventures. Back up a generation: the father of those four men, the grandfather I had never known. West Point graduate in 1912, buck-lieutenant in WWI France, survivor of Chateau-Thierry and Belleau Wood, career Army officer between the World Wars when a career in the military was about as prestigious and lucrative as working down a coal mine. Retired a Colonel. I had ancestors on both sides in the Civil War. Ancestors in the Whiskey Rebellion...both sides. Now *there's* a little-known American conflict that evoked strong moral positions...and nearly destroyed the fledgling nation. I had ancestors in the Revolution, both in the Continental Army and in backwood bands of irregulars. Probably had ancestors in the Scots Regiments brought over to help suppress those Damned Revolutionary Colonialist upstarts, damn their damned eyes! Don't forget Red-Legs Greaves, f'chrissake! A pirate so cunning the British finally gave up trying to catch him and offered him Letters of Marque to conduct seaborne depredations against the Spanish and French. Notably chivalrous to the ladies. Never killed a man who didn't need killing. Hospitable to those he captured, while waiting patiently for their ransoms to be delivered. In later life, Greaves lived to great old age, and served for many years as Governor of Barbados. Died in his bed at age eighty-four. Revered upon his passing as a philanthropist and benefactor of the Church. What a man! Of Scots ancestry, naturally! Clan MacLeod of Lewis.

Were my renowned ancestors *heroes*? *War-lovers*? None of the ones I knew personally. None of the rest, if my dad's recollections were accurate. What were they then? Americans (well…those who weren't, were *Scots*!) who knew that on occasion, what an individual believes in and wishes for must be put on hold. That sometimes it becomes necessary to suck it up and do what might be personally distasteful – even contrary to one's personal principles – *but has to be done anyway*. The greater good demands it, or perhaps the public will as expressed by the law of the land demands it…even if the public will is misguided or unpopular. In order to live with yourself as a man, you've got to suck it up. Do the hard thing. Pay the price of being a citizen by submerging your own personal resolve, at least temporarily. Then, when you get back, if you survive, you exert your vote and your opinion and your own personal will to the full extent of whatever vigor you possess, in support of your principles no matter how radical. *That's* how that First Amendment thing works. I found myself thinking along these lines, although knowing full well that many intelligent and well-intentioned people would not find my conclusions acceptable themselves. I found myself *loathing* the facile suggestions with which I was being bombarded as to how I might avoid the unpleasantness of the Draft, offered up largely by those who were not currently in the crosshairs, who seemed to be somehow proof from induction, while it was I who held in my hands that letter from the Draft Board, God bless 'em. I found myself thinking more and more of that archetypal American war-hero: Joshua Lawrence Chamberlain. If you are unaware of this man's influence on the events of American History, please remedy that shortcoming as soon as possible. Here was a man who sucked it up, put his strong personal moral principles on hold, and did what was expected of him…and, ultimately, a whole lot more. Elle and I had long talks about what likely awaited me. And when the day came that I had to get on the bus for the Induction Center, we were both fairly-much at peace with what was about to transpire.

I packed a very small suitcase of personal items. Elle drove me to the Induction Center. She kissed me goodbye. I felt like I was going to get ferried across the Styx in the next few minutes and never come back. There were antiwar protesters in front of the building who tried to convince me to turn around and walk away at this, the last minute. They had instructional brochures. Shoot your toe off, flee to Sweden, conscientiously object…I'd heard all those before. Honestly, I gave that course a moment's thought. Then I went ahead and pushed through the glass doors.

It was dazzling how quickly and efficiently the staff swept me into the process. Within five minutes, I was standing on a painted, numbered square of floor-tile, my right hand raised, repeating phrase-by-phrase a solemn oath that made me a recruit in the United States Army. Three minutes later, I was taking the first of two dozen arcane tests intended to figure out just what specific kind of a recruit they might make of me – after I survived eight weeks of Basic Training. *Assuming* I survived.

Onto a chartered Greyhound bus. Muted conversations with fellow recruits, as dazed as I was. Long three-hour drive northward. Then through the ominous gate of a sprawling Army fort I had blithely driven past on the Interstate, innumerable times, with scant knowledge of what lay inside that barbwired vastness. I expected to read the words *ARBEIT MACHT FREI* on the arch above the gateway. But that would have been just a bit too surreal.

Herded into a barracks by fairly cordial NCOs. A briefing on what to expect: Find a rack and stow your gear. Smoke 'em if you got 'em, but only outside. No butts on the floor, goddammit …use the red butt-cans! Fall out for dinner when a corporal came to collect us. Not a squeak after lights-out. Get some sleep, gentlemen…tomorrow's going to be a big day. Biggest day in your pathetic lives so far.

The crisply-uniformed briefer executed a sharp about-face and left us stewing in our juices.

The next day was all about tests and assessments until two

o'clock. One particular test I rather enjoyed. It was the Army's own language aptitude evaluation. We were issued a sealed pamphlet, a pencil, and a scantron sheet – one of those things for automated multiple-choice test scorings where you bubble-in a little circle? Sorry…everyone in the galaxy knows what a scantron is. Imagine my surprise when I broke the seal on the pamphlet, right on the dot of the corporal's crisp command, and discovered that the first several multiple-choice questions were based on the following sentence, near as I can recall:

La aviadilo forlasi tri bomboj.

Why hell! This was *Esperanto*! Please don't imagine that I possessed any fluency in Esperanto whatsoever, but at least I'd heard of the language! In one of my high school English classes, a guy I knew got up and delivered a short speech on the artificial tongue. He read out a very amusing paragraph in Esperanto, and I don't think there was any sixteen-year-old in the classroom who didn't get the gist. I'd taken four years of French, and was moderately fluent. There was even that hellish semester of *Russian* in my checkered University past! In the first five seconds of the thirty minutes allocated for the Language Aptitude Evaluation, I figured out that I had two things going for me: number one, I probably had more exposure to linguistic structure -- you know, conjugating them verbs, declining them modifiers? Gender and syntax and all that jazz? – than your usual US Army bootcamp inductee, and number two, the mere awareness of the *existence* of Esperanto had yanked the carpet of dread and mystery out from under this exam! I put pencil to scantron-sheet and got going.

After the pamphlets and scantrons were collected, we sat silent as statues at rigid attention while a cluster of uniformed enlisted types ran the answer sheets through a big automatic scoring machine. Scores came up in bright red numerals on the front of the machine. One guy retrieved each scantron as it came spitting out of the machine, called out the score and the inductee's name, wrote the score on the scantron, then punched a reset button on the machine. Another guy wrote the score on an arcane form, evidently a personal tracking-sheet that was intended to follow each and every one of us around through all the tests and examinations of the induction procedure. A third guy wrote the score into a large loose-leaf ledger. Then a fourth guy would call out the name of the recruit just evaluated, who would by golly hop-to if he knew what was good for him, advance to the front desk and collect the bad news on his graded scantron. My turn came around. What was written on the top of the sheet looked something like this: *28/60* ...Twenty-eight out of sixty. A trifle less than 50%. Not so good. I pivoted to return to my seat. Then I noticed that there were mechanically-daubed red marks, courtesy of that scoring-machine, next to the "wrong" answers. There were only TWO red marks. My score should have been FIFTY-eight.

"Uhhh...pardon me, corporal. There seems to be a mistake. Shouldn't this be fifty-eight?" What possessed me to actually speak up, I will not ever know.

Intensely irked, the corporal yanked the scantron back from me. He gave it the briefest of once-overs. "Nope. Twenty-eight."

"But—"

"Listen, you goddamned puke-smelling maggot! Average score on this test is SEVEN! You gotta twenty-eight so just be goddamn proud of your crappy self. Now get back to that desk and shut the fuck up! Jesus Christ! Fifty-eight?...*nobody* gets fifty-eight!" I had an instant's flash of that corporal, but in a tall, bright-green, furry busby and a droopy walrus-mustache, saying "Wizard?...*nobody* gets to see the Wizard!" but I held my tongue.

The little Language Aptitude Evaluation fiasco probably cost me a cushy appointment to the Army's Language School in Monterey, California, a thirty-seven week intensive program that immersed the trainee in 24/7 studies of some language or another. I'd come out with astounding fluency in *German*! Or heck, maybe they'd figure I already had a jumpstart on *Russian*, and train me up some more in that! No...it was almost certain to be Vietnamese. Well no sense obsessing about it...Language School wasn't going to happen. But the valuable lesson I learned was that it wasn't going to do much good trying to stick up for myself against the stacked deck I was facing, at least for the next eight weeks. If a minor functionary gave me a random made-up score just because he had an instant's trouble believing his own eyes, then that's the way it was going to be played. Just keep my own counsel and take the lumps handed me. Oh, and maybe maintain a low profile.

At two o'clock a Specialist-Sixth Class came to collect us. A few of us had learned through the incredible military grapevine that the correct though distinctly non-polite term for this rank was "Speedy-Six". We were arranged by height in rows and columns. We were run through half an hour of agonizing calisthenics, until everyone was flowing with sweat. Except the Speedy-Six. Then we were marched – no, I'm wrong…we were flat-out *run* – over to a small building where we were ordered to form up in a number of lines, queued on a number of doors. Inside each mysterious door was a chair and a barber with a savage, merciless set of electric clippers. There went every scrap of hair off of every head. One's self-regard. One's uniqueness. One's very personality. Now an untidy mess lying on the barbershop floor. We were obliged to *pay* two bucks for this service.

Then it was another two-mile run to a huge long building where a line of very aggravated civilian employees equipped us with fatigue pants, shirts, underwear, socks, two pairs of black combat boots, hats, helmets, coats, gloves, sheets and pillowcases, toiletries, hankies, belts, boot-polish, and a big olive-drab barracks bag into which all this stuff was supposed to be crammed. Precise fitting of the garments was accomplished by having them thrown at your face, along with the vilest of curses. Then once more into the line, dear friends, and another high-speed run over to the barracks in which we had spent the previous night…only this time, humping those miserable stuffed ungainly heavy barracks bags.

The uniform of the day was described to us by a PFC, in an intemperate voice punctuated with curses. We were given five minutes to effect the change. Our civilian garb was to be stuffed into the suitcases we'd brought with us, and the suitcases locked up somewhere irretrievable for the next eight weeks. Recall, please, that a sadistic Speedy-Six had made certain our last civvie outfit would be saturated in our own reeking sweat before this latest development transpired.

And so it went. Transfer to the Training Company barracks. Introduction to the hideous sadists who were to be our Drill Instructors for the next eight weeks. Master Sergeant Dean, First Sergeant Draco. Top Sergeant Moreton. The Top was a cold *eminence grise* who never cursed nor raised his voice, invariably formal and reasonable. And implacably hostile. His icy glance was enough to stop a boot's heart in his chest. We were warned that these gentlemen were not to be called "Sir", because they were not goddamned officers, goddamnit! They were US Army NCOs, and, therefore, close kin to goddamn deities! They were to be called "Drill Sergeant" or "Drill Instructor". "DI" was acceptable, but only barely. Oh, and actual goddamned officers were to be saluted, respected, and tremblingly obeyed. They were all pretty badass hombres, this bunch, but the most insane of the lot was a diminutive Filipino named Sergeant Yoyo. A hundred twenty pounds, five-feet-two in his combat boots…but all of it gristle and snake-venom. God help you if you got that absurd name wrong.

M16s issued, to be cleaned into spotlessness, then transferred to the company armory. Better not forget your weapon number! We got packs. Webgear. Bayonets. Shelter-halves and entrenching tools. There was no mistaking it, by six o'clock on that momentous day, I was *in the Army*. What I'd write Elle about all this was a moot point, because I was too exhausted to lift a pencil.

One last ordeal. Just before chow-time, us boots were made to fall in on a series of numbers out in the asphalt quad, numbers we'd grow as familiar with as the facial features of our dear sainted mothers. Roll was taken. About half us boots didn't answer-up with sufficient crispness and were assigned pushups to do, right then and there on the asphalt. I got fifty, which actually wasn't too bad. Then, in order to be admitted to the mess hall and a waiting nutritious dinner, each boot had to climb a platform and execute the transit of a torture-rack called the Horizontal Ladder, swinging from rung to rung like an Orang-Utan. Two yards below our dangling feet, a pit of slime. We'd already been warned that we were responsible for maintaining our combat boots in glossy, spit-shined condition at all times, so there was penalty on top of penalty for failing to make it across. There were at least fifty rungs. I made four. No worries…that was about average on that first day. I crept from the slimepit and glooshed in to dinner.

We discovered that our 48-trainee platoon, which bore the designation of Platoon One, Alpha Company, Second Battalion, Second Training Brigade, or One-Alpha-Two-Two, had been gifted with a virtual clone of the character "Zero" from Beetle Bailey. An amiable kid, no more than seventeen years old, with a very low I.Q. and absolutely no good sense whatsoever. By rights, a person like this had no business playing with loaded guns. But I was beginning to gain a respect for the Army's inscrutable methods and sly training techniques. 'Zero' had been put in our platoon for a good reason. He was so accident-prone and clueless that the rest of us had to look out for him. When he screwed up (which was frequently), it was likely the whole platoon wound up doing an extra two hours of drill and calisthenics on his behalf. His presence made us protect our own…made us knit together into more of a team, to keep our Zero from screwing up. I would not be surprised to find that the US Army actively recruits Zeros, and carefully places one in each training platoon. I never met a fellow enlistee who *hadn't* had a Zero of his own in Basic Training. Surprisingly, the subterfuge actually worked.

…Most of the time.

Sometime during the first week, our boy Zero came slouching into the barracks in that blissful forty-five minutes of time-off at the end of each grueling day, before we were bellowed out to the assembly area and the dreaded Horizontal Ladder preceding dinner. He looked as if he was going to cry.

"Hey what's up, guy?" someone asked.

Zero gazed about mournfully. "I'm in trouble! Gotta report to the DI's staff-room after dinner."

"What did you do?"

"Called that little Mexican DI 'Sergeant YooHoo'."

Oh crap. That was serious. Not just the name…that 'Mexican' *faux pas,* if ever Sergeant Yoyo had gotten wind of it. Not an

45

acceptable mistake, to the mind of any patriotic Filipino. Zero disappeared after chow. Long after lights-out, sometime around eleven p.m., he slunk back into the darkened barracks. Concerned buddies began to ask what had transpired, but a 140-decibel voice from out in the hallway bellowed "Shut the fuck up and go to sleep!" We complied, naturally. We could hear Zero climbing into his upper bunk, then softly sobbing himself into an uneasy slumber, poor guy.

Our training proceeded. Military instructors are highly skilled. Their students give them the fullest attention. If not, the inattentive students are persuaded to regret the day they were conceived. Every single hourlong presentation, from hand-grenades to venereal-disease prevention, from map reading to dental hygiene, was preceded by the exact-same sentence:

"Gentlemen, this particular block of instruction is the *most important information* you will receive in your entire eight weeks of Basic Training!"

Somewhere during the third week, a whip-thin black sergeant-first-class, just home from the jungles of Southeast Asia, gave us a morning's instruction on finding our way around unfamiliar terrain with a hand compass and a topographic map. Ah, this was good stuff! MY area of expertise! As a student and then as a practicing forester, I'd made a daily living from topographic maps and compasses for the better part of three years. So when the instructor got a particular statement of fact *wrong*, I felt it my duty to offer a polite correction. At issue is how you tell whether the contour lines indicate you are going UPHILL or going DOWNHILL. He had based his facts on the orientation of the contours' convexity. To illustrate, he called the trainees' attention to a particular grid square on the maps in front of each of us. "Which way does the terrain slope as you move to the Northwest?" he bellowed rhetorically. "Co-RECT! It slopes uphill!"

I found my hand involuntarily going up. I was recognized from the podium. "I believe you'd be going downhill, Drill Sergeant," I offered a trifle timidly.

46

"No. Uphill!"

"Well…uh…Drill Instructor, wouldn't that put the Puget Sound at a higher elevation than the Fort? You'd think the ocean water would all run toward the southeast down that slope you're talking about and flood us out…" There was a very light ripple of *sotto voce* laughter from the trainees who caught on to the little point I was making. I swear it was not my purposeful intention to make the Drill Instructor look foolish.

I was cursed for my ignorance. I was exemplified as a moron who had not grasped the simplest concept. I was informed that of course the Fort was at a lower elevation than Puget Sound, that if I cared to look and wasn't such an idiot, I would see that there was a large berm along the shore holding the water back. I turned red, but I learned yet another lesson about the military mindset: you cannot successfully question higher authority, even when you have a convincing argument to back you up. Facts, if they don't exist, will be invented on the spot to discredit your critique. Ah well, no great harm done this time, other than possibly reinforcing some misinformation in the minds of a parcel of recruits. I concluded that I'd love to have a nice chat with a military historian about the price of obstinacy in the face of facts. Save it for later.

On another occasion, my voluntarily stepping up to the microphone worked out a little better. I'd started Basic Training on the twelfth of October, and for the first couple weeks, the weather held mild and fine. Then, about the first of November it started to rain. A *cold* rain. A *lot* of it. All day long. Didn't matter…we hiked and did physical training and fired-off round after round of M16 ammo on the rifle range, even in the pour-down rain. After all…we were told it rained quite a bit in Viet Nam, where all our sorry asses were certain to be bound. Well, we had a three-day field exercise coming up, during which we would bivouac under primitive conditions out in the woods somewhere. One afternoon, in preparation for this, Sergeant Yoyo assembled us all out in a big mown grassfield to learn how to put up two-man military puptents. He had us squat Indian-fashion in the sopping grass, all of us burdened-down with our weapons and webgear and a bunch of rattly, flappy field equipment strapped to it. Each trainee carried, among his equipment, a canvas shelter-half, a single collapsible tent pole, and half a dozen steel tent stakes.

"Attention, young troops," orated Sgt. Yoyo. "This will certainly be the absolute most important hour of instruction you will receive in the entire course of your eight weeks of Basic Training." His flint-hard eyes dared anybody to doubt him. "Soooo..." he locked his hands in the small of his back and strutted left and right like a banty rooster. "Which of you sorry excuses for trainees would like to show the rest of you crap-eating maggots how to put up a two-man military canvas shelter, Airborne-Ranger fashion?"

My hand twitched up into the air. My brain had seemingly taken French Leave for the moment. Hadn't I *learned*? NEVER volunteer!

Yoyo hissed my name with a reptilian smile. "Okay, young troop! The class is yours." He took his ease a little way back, and prepared to be entertained by my fumblings. His plan, of course, was to have me illustrate how NOT to put up a military canvas shelter, Ranger fashion. While I worked, he was doubtlessly rehearsing all the obscene, insulting names I was in for.

But the thing is, I'd put up tents just like this about ten thousand times. When I was a kid, I'd gotten into the Boy Scouts. Correction...back up three years. I'd gotten into the *Cub* Scouts. *Then* the Boy Scouts. I will not apologize. I had a lot of fun, scouting...and I learned a lot. I stuck with it for years. Earned every rank there was, right up to and including Eagle – Court of Honor, August 1963, age of sixteen. Our troop had had Army-surplus shelter-halves exactly like the one strapped into my webgear, and I'd put the things up and taken them down in all kinds of conditions, at least ten thousand times.

I shucked my webgear. I carefully set my faithful M16 -- Betsy-Lou -- on top. I unstrapped my shelter half. I rolled it out and unfolded it flat. I clicked together my single collapsible tent pole. I tossed steel tent pegs down the line, so they'd lie ready-at-hand along what would become the left-hand outside edge of the tent. "This is half a tent," I said. "Every man has one...that's why

they are designated 'TWO-MAN shelter, canvas, olive-drab'."
Jesus, I was even *sounding* like a DI! "Zero, let me have your tent-half." The doofus did a creditable job of unstrapping his shelter-half in quick-time, and I unrolled it out next to mine. I frog-crawled down the middle, snapping the two halves together along the top seam. I unlimbered my entrenching tool and used it to hammer-in the tent-stakes, four to a side, right down both sides and one more at each of the head and foot apexes of the tent. I drove in an extra stake, head and foot, for the guyropes. I stuck the pin of one of the two tentpoles through the grommet at the head-end and then snapped that end erect. I did the same for the foot-end. I took the first guyrope, passed it once around the waiting stake, and said, "Watch carefully, gentlemen. This is called a tautline hitch. Cross the loose end over. Two wraps below the crossover, one wrap above, tucked through. All three wraps in the same direction. Simple as pie. Slide this hitch up the guyrope. It allows you to tighten the guyrope at liberty. That will pull the tent nice and tight. The hitch will not slip so long as the rope remains taut. Easy to release when you take the tent down. Private Zero, you do the other end." So simple that even a moronic doofus could do it, as Zero capably demonstrated. "Spread out that waterproof groundcover before you unroll your sleeping bags," I lectured, getting into it. "When you and your buddy crawl in, both your heads need to be up at one end. Sleep head-to-toe and you'll thrash around in a terrible tangle if you have to get out of there quickly in the dark. And besides, you'd have to smell each other's feet all night. Stow your muddy boots and packs down by your feet. Weapons safed, right there handy between the two of you. They'll keep you from rolling over and trying to smooch your buddy in your dreams." A riffle of laughter. "Don't touch the tent fabric once you're inside. If you do, the rainwater will wick through and drip on your ass. Keep the flaps open a little bit, even if it's cold or raining. If you don't have any ventilation, your breath will sweat-up the tent and you might as well be sleeping out in the rain. Also, your buddy probably farts a lot." A bit more laughter. I stepped back from a drum-tight tent. It actually takes longer to *describe* doing the job than it took to *do* the job.

Yoyo mumbled my name three or four times, amazed. "Where in HELL did you learn to do that?" he asked, astounded.

"Boy Scouts."

The platoon erupted in raucous laughter. They didn't get to do that much. While they laughed, Sgt. Yoyo snapped to attention, executing a respectful, militarily-precise salute! I returned the salute and he ordered-arms just as the guys ran out of amusement.

God-DAMN, that felt good!

Days in Basic Training crawl by with a reluctance that makes you think of Einstein and the General Theory of Relativity. Has the entire world somehow started flying *backward* at relativistic velocities, so that time dilates the wrong way? Each hour lasts days, each day crawls by with the speed of a chilly snail on top of a glacier. Those eight grueling weeks took a lifetime to run their course.

But I gradually began to notice several things. I – and each one of my buddies – was becoming hard. Rock-hard. Indefatigable. Canny, knowledgeable. An expert marksman. Fast. Durable. Strong. Friedrich Nietzsche had the right of it...Basic wasn't killing us – quite – but it was making us stronger. Do you remember that Horizontal Ladder? By Week Four, fifty rungs was nothing – *nothing*! I never fell in the slime anymore. I'd started to work on *how fast* I could brachiate down the line, giving no thought any longer as to whether or not I'd make it. Since only one trainee at a time went down the Ladder, the DI's – and all the trainees! – yelled and screamed for each guy to hurry the hell up. Chow was waiting – probably getting cold! Zero had always had difficulty under that kind of pressure. It took him until halfway through Week Six to negotiate the full distance. Then the day came when he went all the way down doubletime, fifty rungs, *then turned and swung hand-over-hand back*! The volume of verbal abuse became deafening. Returning to a position a couple rungs before the starting-point, Zero spread his dangling legs and emitted a resounding fart at the booing, cursing mob. Then he turned again, dangling one-handed for a moment, and unhurriedly chimpanzeed his way across to a well-deserved mess-hall meal.

One hundred fifty rungs!

Yeah well we were getting stronger. No surprise there. But in addition, we were gaining in the ability to function as a team, a potentially *lethal* team. To watch out for each other as if by instinct. To think and act as if wired together. You know that Army recruiting ad on television, "Be an Army of ONE!" What baloney. Men in combat have to mesh, have to think about their teammates, have to be prepared to defend one another, and sacrifice if necessary. It has to come natural. Nobody on the planet does this better than Americans. There were times when I thought Basic Training was cruel, or stupid, or transparent in its little psychological ploys. That little subterfuge of Good DI/Bad DI – gimme a break! But it *worked*. Worked on me, worked on forty-seven other trainees in my platoon. It was all simulation, but not by very much. By week eight, I was soooo ready for it to be over!

On the last day, in the last hour, we fell into formation to await a special handout. Each of us was to receive our orders and Military Occupational Specialties – MOS's -- for advanced training, along with a fistful of cash to get us home for two weeks' leave. Also, air tickets to our advanced-training bases. A folder of papers that tracked our health, catalogued our test scores, and documented the accomplishments of our training…our "permanent record" which we were warned to guard with our very lives and deliver up to the administrator at our next duty station. And a packet of nice studio-photos showing each of us in Dress-Greens, looking like real soldiers. That's pretty much what we'd become.

While we stood around at-ease, waiting for our names to come up, our DIs passed among us, as friendly as old chums. They shook hands and congratulated us by our names, sharing a laugh over some awkwardness or naivete we'd each manifested, back there at the beginning, back when they believed that not one of us scum-sucking fly maggots would amount to anything like soldier material. Here was a surprise: his terrifying façade completely crumbled, the most charm and bonhomie came flowing out of *Sgt. Yoyo*! It was obvious that at the beginning of our training cycle, Yoyo had drawn the short straw. He'd only been playacting the role of insanely, unpredictably Bad DI!

Passing out the order packets was Top Sergeant Mackenroe. An NCO with a face like a pit bull. Musculature to rival a gorilla on steroids. Flat-affect eyes with no joy in them. More service stripes down his sleeve than I had socks in my barracks-bag. Airborne Ranger. Light infantry weapons and demolition specialist. Three tours of duty in Viet Nam in the years prior to that December of 1970...*combat* tours. He was the archetypal tough career-man. We trainees hadn't seen much of Sergeant Mackenroe – he was primarily the company's administrative and logistic liaison -- but he was a daunting, awe-inspiring presence in the company's office spaces. Everyone knew who he was, and everyone trod softly in his presence. When he called my name and I stepped forward to receive my orders, my salute was a little shaky with trepidation.

He silently perused my documents before handing them over. Then he said my name, flat and cold. "A good soldier," he added. He dragged out that middle word: "A gooooood soldier!"

Was it sarcasm? Insincerety? Some form of mockery? I didn't think so. He wasn't the jocular type. His words sounded like a heartfelt compliment from one who was naturally laconic of speech. But...*was I a good soldier*? *Me*? My mind flashed back to all those heavy thoughts I'd had about the difficulty of duty flying in the face of one's personal wishes, in those last days before I'd reported for induction. I thought about Joshua Lawrence Chamberlain, a well-respected professor of religion and philosophy at Bowdoin College in Maine. In 1861, Chamberlain had put his life on hold, temporarily closed the book on his personal feelings, and enlisted in the Union Army over the express objections of his family. His college president had refused to give him leave of absence for military service, but Chamberlain had enlisted anyway. Two years later, his personal heroism and quick, unconventional action had singlehandedly prevented the Union line at Gettysburg from being overrun and folded up on its far left flank by the Rebs, and probably saved the Union from a massive defeat, twenty thousand additional casualties, and shameful ignominy. The entire outcome of the Civil War may very well

52

have pivoted on Chamberlain's audacious actions. Sergeant Mackenroe had access to my records…he knew I was not the stuff of heroes, would never become a career man in this Army of his. He also knew I was almost twenty-four years old in a platoon of seventeen- and eighteen-year-olds, the "old man" of the outfit. He knew I had a beloved wife back home, who received a bountiful $86 a month as a dependent's stipend, instead of the love, comfort and support of her husband. He knew I'd been the fortunate recipient of more education than any one of that entire platoonful of other guys, and had left a viable career to serve in a time of war. He knew I'd sucked it up and got on the bus when my Draft Board, God bless 'em, had sent me their letter. I was the archetype of who the Army needed, to make its mission sustainable. Citizen soldiers, giving it their best effort, no matter the personal cost. And I hadn't complained very much, and I hadn't been too much trouble, and I'd learned my lessons, and I'd improved remarkably in just about every measurement of stamina and ability, and I'd done a pretty good job becoming a strong, skilled soldier. A good soldier, indeed. Those three mild words of praise, coming from this lion of a man, seriously choked me up.

I glanced down at the assignment orders he'd handed me. USAINTS, Fort Holabird, Maryland. Specialty assignment: Ninety-Six Bravo. Nine weeks' advanced training. "Top," I stammered. "What's a Ninety-Six Bravo? And what's USAINTS?"

He puzzled over that one. "Beats hell out of me. Just a minute…" He stepped back to a desk and thrashed around in a drawer. Thumbed through a manual. Came strolling on back.

"Intelligence Analyst," he said. "USAINTS is the United States Army INTelligence School."

8
My Strenuous Mental Exertions at USAINTS

Elle met me at the training compound on graduation day. When she flung herself on me, I could sense a ripple of envy sweep through the guys of One-Alpha-Two-Two. Wasn't there an Old-Testament commandment about coveting your buddy's amazing, gorgeous, sexy, vivacious wife?

She had come up to the Fort twice before. On Visitor's Day two weeks into my Basic tour, and then again for a visit at five weeks. It was a long, long drive for a two-hour visit. The arrangement for wives and sweethearts was not very satisfying: a big, cold room decked out with the meagerest of military decorative touches in an attempt to make it a more intimate space. Upholstered chairs in pairs. Fabric partitions intended to give a bit of privacy. Plastic flowers in vases. Coffee and soda and cookies that not one yearning couple really had time for. On the wall, a big implacable clock that ticked off the seconds of those two hours, while desperately I grasped both her hands like a man drowning. We were permitted to talk to our hearts' content... inconsequentialities about the amusing difficulties of our respective lives. We were permitted to kiss. The officers who monitored Visitor's Day did their very best to avert their eyes. Well all that was nice, of course, but so far less than sweeping her out of this dreary place and making off to something resembling that Eden in which we'd spent all those blissful months since our wedding day. During the eight weeks just concluded, between those two painfully-short visits and the steady stream of letters, always upbeat and newsy and redolent with Elle's special perfume-scent, she managed to keep me afloat through the lowest lows of Basic Training.

Now we had two weeks' leave before I'd have to get on a plane headed for Fort Holabird, Maryland. We drove to Eastern Oregon up the snow-dusted Columbia Gorge, and spent a few days with a couple of dear friends who'd lived on that idyllic Ranger District with us, but recently had moved to Pendleton. One icy-cold day a week before Christmas the four of us drove out into the far reaches of Godforsaken Eastern Washington to a hot-springs. Soaking and frolicking in boiling water while our breaths darted out in frosty mist was a delightful experience in sensory contrast. After that nice visit, we drove two hundred miles back to Elle's shabby little trailer up on cinderblocks. While I was at boot camp, Elle had come into ownership of a dog. Reddy, a very large, very male Doberman Pinscher. I had lived in dread of my first meeting with Reddy. Dobermans have a fearful reputation. I imagined he'd bonded with my adorable wife...who wouldn't? I imagined he'd take one look at me the first time I put a hand anywhere near her, growl ferally, and proceed to rip out my throat. I was a little off-the-mark. On first meeting, Reddy took one look at me, barked happily, and proceeded to lick my face from chin to hairline. I believe he thought Elle was okay and everything, but he had instantly decided I was Jove Himself, down from Valhalla for the purpose of bringing light, love and order into his heretofore humdrum doggie life. He set about worshipping the very ground my shadow fell across. He went on like that until the end of his days. Oh, and kindly don't believe everything you hear about Doberman Pinschers.

Next we drove 500 miles south to spend some time with my parents. Reddy squatted in the back-seat of Elle's nearly-derelict Comet as it gasped southward, lolling out the window whenever we cranked it down and gave him the opportunity. My parents were as quirky as ever. My dad, who back in his salad days had been through everything I was experiencing, actually *wept* when I stepped out of the car...something I had never witnessed in my life. I was thirty pounds lighter than the last time he'd seen me, tightly-muscled, quarter-inch fuzz of hair on my scalp. Like had been done to him, I had been turned into a soldier -- in a time of war.

Elle and I drove out into the countryside or over to the coast every day. We walked along the beach while the spent ocean rollers purled and creamed around our ankles. We strolled the zoo. We had picnics while bundled up in coats and mittens, in the icy wintertime park above the University, revisiting haunts of our college days. Christmas came and went. Then the two weeks were up. We did not succeed in conceiving a child over that two-week leave, Elle and I. But not from lack of trying.

She drove me to the airport. Kissed me good-bye once again while holding back her tears. In my inexperience, I thought that Advanced Training would be just a whole lot more of the agony of Basic Training. I mounted the steps to that 747 like a murderer mounting the gallows staircase. But the flight attendant asked me if I'd like to ride in one of the unoccupied First Class seats. That was so kind of her! And the luxury removed some of the sting from that five-hour eastward flight.

Fort Holabird turned out to be a small, grubby military post. A noisome waterway made up the eastern boundary: Colgate Creek. Three hundred yards upstream was a manufacturing plant which was one of the principal sources of the distinctive odors on the air. It turned out to be a Lever Brothers factory. That made a certain sense…either the creek had been named after the toothpaste, or the toothpaste had been named after the creek. Colgate Creek always seemed to carry a thick float of white foam, as if sixteen thousand factory workers were up there brushing their teeth all day long, testing product…and spitting in the water. A second component of industrial aroma was contributed by a factory that produced brewer's yeast in wholesale batches. On reflection, that yeast could easily have been the source of Colgate Creek's foam coating.

In spite of the air quality, Fort Holabird was the US Military's focal-point for training in intelligence. All service branches were represented. Officers were trained there, or brought in for refresher courses or briefings. Allied personnel abounded, and we enlisted trainees had to study diagrams of British, West German, French, Greek, South Korean, and South Vietnamese officer insignia. All those pesky officers required saluting, whenever encountered out-of-doors. The old advice to salute it if it moves was not too far off the mark.

The day I arrived at Fort Holabird was my twenty-fourth birthday. Big deal. I schlurped strawberry ice cream for dessert at lunch and sang myself Happy Birthday very quietly. No gifts, please.

A pleasant discovery in my first half-hour on base was that I could be free to relax! Basic Training had been the universal ordeal…but now I was past that. My nine weeks at Holabird would be an "at-ease" time, by comparison. There would be a few duties, of course, and an adequate amount of military rigor – like that saluting thing. But I was not going to have to slink around in fear. I could go off-base anytime I wanted, after hours, and spend my weekends in the fleshpots and tinny bars of Baltimore if I wished, sloshing down alcoholic liquids, or trying to cultivate temporary friendships with scary-looking barflies, or getting fleeced by the usual set of parasites who frequent the neighborhood of military bases.

Within the first day at Holabird, I acquired a lifelong friend. Wes hailed from New Braunfels, Texas, not too far from San Antonio, but had just completed Basic in Washington State, just like me. It turned out that his training company was Bravo-two-two, just across the asphalt assembly-yard from my company's barracks! We exchanged observations.

"Why were they so hard on you guys?" I asked. I'd seen the Bravo-company DI's driving their sweat-streaming trainees like galley-slaves.

"Wull, we-all wondered why they were agoin' so *easy* on you fellers! But—"

"Shit, man! It didn't *feel* like easy!"

"I was gonna say, but one of the DI's tole a guy in my squad that Alpha-two-two and Charlie-two-two were agettin' special handling…like a expeeriment or somethin'. Word is, within a year or so there's gonna be no more draft. All-volunteer Army, they're acallin' it. Ifn they don't go a little easier on the trainees, they's not gonna get no volunteers a-tall!"

In the first week, I got called into the commandant's office. Orders were handed to me declaring I was hereby promoted to Private E-2. So was Wes and about six or seven other buck-privates. Two weeks later, the same rigmarole happened again and four of us got bumped up to Private First-Class. Wes and I made the cut again.

Well Wes and I proceeded to mow a swath through our Ninety-Six Bravo training. Intelligence Analysis school was like a long series of brain-teasers and mental exercises, designed to hone the ability to spot patterns within overwhelming masses of observable data. This is how 'data' got turned into 'intelligence', and the mental exercise was right down my alley. In spite of his droll west-Texan aw-shucks diction, Wes was one of the most intelligent individuals I'd ever encountered. He and I had a natural synergistic tendency, so we partnered-up on study tasks whenever possible. Like me, Wes had a wife back home...but also a little boy just one year old. Two weeks into our course, his wife sent him a letter saying she was filing for divorce and intending to marry some guy she'd met at work when he was in his first weeks of basic training. Accompanying the letter was a bunch of forms for Wes to sign, then return to his erstwhile wife's attorney. Just as a capper, she demanded Wes surrender parental rights for his son...her 'fiance' was going to adopt him as his own little boy. Sweet, huh? First time in my life, someone leaned on me for comfort and strength...but we got Wes through it, more or less.

There was one particular instructor who, like Sgt. Yoyo, had taken on the role of badass nemesis. Or maybe he was just naturally like that. A Marine. A Marine *officer*. By name, Captain Cameron. Another of those hard-as-nails Scots, did you notice? Early-on, Captain Cameron challenged our fifty-person class of Ninety-Six Bravo trainees to spend some of our time-off voluntarily solving a series of puzzles and breaking a series of sample codes, just to hone our nascent abilities. "I doubt any of you Army pukes have the skill to succeed," he opined. "Or the gumption to even try."

Well naturally this was a red flag waved in front of a bull for Wes and me. Since four-man teams were the order of the day, we drafted privates Monk and Horner to throw in with us.

The first of Captain Cameron's challenges was a puzzle involving five fictitious enemy units arrayed side-by-side across the fictitious line-of-battle in a fictitious forest. We were presented with a short list of intelligence findings that had been garnered about these enemies:

Colonel Pang's men wear red scarves.

The troops carrying bazookas prefer night-envelopment attacks.

The unit to General Woo's left has a leopard as a mascot.

Blue scarves have been spotted on the far right of the enemy's lines.

There are black scarves around the necks of the troops armed with AK47's.

...and so on, for ten or twelve more such statements. At the bottom, the question posed was:

What color scarves do Brigadier Chang's troops wear?

The solution technique was obvious. Set up a matrix of five units. A diagram would be helpful. There were five categories of data: commander's name, scarf color, preferred weapon, preferred attack method, unit mascot. Insert the relational data, use logic and elimination and geometry, and the unknown answer will fall right into our laps.

Well we couldn't get it solved. Around and around we went. The geometry wouldn't work out. After five days, we slunk into Captain Cameron's office, shamefaced and frustrated. "Give us a hint!" we begged.

"Let's hear your logic, boys."

Wes spoke for us. "Wull, them enemies is over there in the woods. We gotta start out with some known fact, get one a them units pinned down. We figger the blue scarves are over here on the right, from this-here fact." He pointed at the list, then at our diagram. "Then there's 80mm mortars raht here in this spot, guys with green scarves. Then there's gotta be—" He went down the line with our diagram and the known facts until it was apparent we were hopelessly scrambled.

"Wait just a damned minute," said the Captain, rather unsympathetically. "Where's General Woo?"

Wes pointed a finger toward the diagram. "Raht here."

"And where's the leopard boys?"

59

Again he pointed. With his left hand, to the position just to his left of General Woo.

"Which direction is them General Woo boys facing, do you suppose? And how about the leopard boys?"

All four of us pondered. Wes spoke out first. He'd just on the instant figured out what idiots we four had been. "T'wards us fellers, most likely," he answered in sheepish tones.

Cameron picked up the assignment paper and scanned down the list of known facts. He quoted Fact Number Three: "The unit to *General Woo's left* has a leopard for a mascot. *General Woo's left,* not *yours*! Get smart, you pathetic Army pukes!" The Marine Captain tossed the fluttering paper back toward Wes and turned his back on us in disgust.

The solution instantly reassembled itself correctly before our minds' eyes. I realized the significance of the mistake I and my cronies had made. It was a mistake a lot bigger than leopards and red scarves. We had failed to look at the problem from the correct point-of-view. That bonehead mistake was a valuable lesson, and I have been careful all the rest of my days to refrain from repeating it. Orchestrating this type of embarrassing mistake was the very nature of intelligence training. The successful ones among us took ownership of our errors, learned from our stupidity, and never repeated the same mistake twice.

We worked our way through the rest of Captain Cameron's extra-credit problems with a lot more success. Grudgingly, he accepted our submissions and tendered grumpy, reluctant Marine-Corps half-ass compliments on each of our efforts. We got down to the last problem. The instructions were verbal and terse, right from the Captain's mouth. "Break the Aggressor Code."

The US Department of Defense, sometime after World War II, had invented the Aggressor. This was a fictitious enemy, for use in war games, simulations, intelligence exercises. The Aggressor was a bad dude. Part Nazi, part godless Soviet commie, part Red Chinese, part Viet Cong guerrilla. In pseudo Aggressor history, these meanies had treacherously invaded the Western Hemisphere through British Columbia and Washington State in 1958, and we'd been fighting a rearguard action against them for twelve years...drawn-out combat by sea, by land, in the air, in space. There had been thermonuclear exchanges. There were Aggressor uniforms, Aggressor religious and political and economic doctrine, an Aggressor language – interestingly, *Esperanto*! -- mock Aggressor weaponry. It wouldn't have surprised me if there weren't actual Aggressor aircraft and panzers stuck away at a military base somewhere. I *know* that one time I saw the Aggressor Circle-Trigon symbol painted on Armored Personnel Carriers used in field exercises at Fort Meade. At Fort Holabird, we mainly got to work with a handful of documents and publications ostensibly chronicling the ongoing warfare between the Aggressor and the "good guys", i.e. NATO and the US military. Among these publications was the Aggressor Order of Battle Manual.

There was an appendix to the OB Manual, showing the names of about three hundred Aggressor military units along with each unit's six-digit coded identity number, used in documents and radio communications to conceal the actual identity of Aggressor units in the field. The information in this Manual appendix represented the sum-total of years of espionage and radio-transmission analysis on the part of our valiant Army intelligence folks. To give an example, the 455th Tank Battalion might have a code of 672218. This was the Aggressor Code we were tasked with breaking. The only helpful hint that the Manual gave was a small footnote stating:

Analysts in the Pentagon believe that the fourth digit of any unit's code- number has something to do with the unit's size.

Well the four of us got right to work. We went through the list in that appendix. Sure enough, all the "Battalions" had a fourth digit of 2. All the "Companies" had a fourth digit of 5. And so forth. In about five minutes, we had a little table for decoding the fourth digit of any code-number to yield the size of any particular Aggressor unit. Now, what about the other five digits?

An inspiration came to me. "Look, guys. All the Aggressor unit identifiers have three parts: a numerical designation, a mission description -- what the unit does for a living, basically -- and a unit size. We've got unit-size pinned down...that takes care of one digit in the six-digit code-number. Notice that we're dealing with less than ten different unit sizes, so a single digit in the code-number is adequate to encode it – Digit Four. There are a maximum of three digits in the unit's numerical designation. We don't yet know which three code-number digits we're looking for there. I'll bet a nickel that one- or two-digit unit numerical designations decode with leading zeros...so the 6th Armored Brigade probably is designated the 006 Armored Brigade. So there gotta be three more code-number digits used for the unit numerical designation. The next thing is I'd be willing to bet another nickel that there are less than one hundred different unit mission descriptions – two more code-number digits for that one, and we don't yet know which two. However, that tidily takes care of the entire six digits. That's *got* to be the way the code works. So let's get to work decoding!"

It took us about an hour and a half. Horner and Monk went off in a corner to work out the unit mission description business. That left Wes and me to deal with the unit numerical designations. By the time we were done, we had it nailed down flat. Unit mission descriptions worked out more orderly than we thought. They fell into a handful of groupings. For example: armored units, infantry combat units, transportation units, support and logistics units, and so forth. Each of these groupings had no more than ten specific mission descriptions within them. Like, Airborne Infantry, Mechanized Infantry, Rapid-Response Infantry, Mountain Infantry, Night-Attack Infantry, and so forth. So, one code-number digit for the grouping, one code-number digit for the specific mission. They were easy to pick out of the uncommitted five digit-positions, and the other two guys quickly had a lookup table drawn up. That only left the remaining three code-number digits for Wes and me to decode into the unit's numerical designation. One of those three digits was a snap to identify, and we easily spotted which of the remaining code digit-positions it was. Here's how that first one decoded: if the code-number digit was a 0, the decoded digit was a 9. If the code-number digit was 1, the digit was 8. And so forth. A simple inverse sequence.

The second of the three digits was a little trickier, but only a little. It was the third digit that was the stumper.

Wes spotted it first. "Wull..." he opined. "Looka here. If the unit-size code-number digit – that's Digit Four, you guys! -- is a ODD number, I'm athinkin' this last digit is agonna decode one way...and ifn it's EVEN, it decodes 'nother way." Well that's exactly the way it worked out! Heck, it wasn't anything but logic and pattern-recognition. We tidied up our writeup, made photocopies, then the four of us marched off to confront Captain Cameron.

He was working late in his office. "What's up, boys?" he asked crisply.

The other three looked at me. So, clearly I'd been elected spokesman. "We broke the Aggressor Code, sir," I responded.

"No you didn't"

"Yes we did...sir."

"Nope. Couldn't have. Can't be done."

"Would you like to see what we got, Captain?"

"Well...okay. I don't have a lot of time."

I laid out our findings. As I described our thinking, his face got more and more amazement to it. Finally he whipped open his well-worn copy of the Aggressor Order of Battle Manual and flipped it open to the code appendix. He tried our methodology on a few unit code-numbers. Each one that decoded properly, he'd mutter a low "god-DAMN!" At Decode Attempt No. Fourteen or so, he brightened. "Aha! This one won't work! Your method is full of shit, gentlemen."

We had already discovered what *he* had just discovered. "Yes sir...there is a certain percentage of unit codes which do not decode correctly. We did not have time to go through the entire appendix – we only had a couple of hours to work on this -- but we sort of did a quick statistical analysis on a pretty good-sized sample...maybe eighty units. We figure about one in twenty doesn't decode right. That's five percent. Two possible explanations have occurred to us. First, what we called Hypothesis 'A'...it seems likely that maybe our intelligence is not 100%

accurate. That 5% represents our screwups, our stupid errors. This is the enemy, after all. You gotta expect they engage in duplicity and disinformation."

"Um…what's the other possible explanation?"

"Well actually this is my personal favorite. Hypothesis 'B'. You will notice on that unit you just found, Captain, that the unit designation number and the unit size decode correctly. What doesn't decode right is the unit mission descriptor. The two digits aren't even in the list."

"And so?"

"Well sir, we believe these units aren't what they'd like us to believe they are. It's likely misdirection. Okay…*simulated* misdirection. Look at that one you picked out: 579th Support Brigade. Those inscrutable aggressive duplicitous Circle-Trigon bastards are having us on. In reality, that's probably the 579th Hideous Chemical-Warfare Brigade or the 579th Military Intelligence Brigade or the 579th Prisoner-of-War Torture Brigade or the 579th Sneaky Bastard Ninja Assassin Brigade. Take that second example I gave: a Military Intelligence unit. We went all the way through the appendix looking at the mission descriptors, and there aren't *any* Military Intelligence units listed. Or Chemical-Warfare units, or Sneaky Ninja Assassin units either. You can't convince me the Aggressor doesn't have anybody doing these jobs. So, maybe for their in-the-clear mission descriptor IDs, they just lump all these sensitive MOS's under "Support" units, or some other general-case duplicitious label, like "Maintenance" or "Logistics", so we won't catch on. Except, the mission descriptor *codes* don't match up. Notice in our lookup table we couldn't come up with a satisfactory two-digit code for "Support" units…because that designation is *always* being used to misguide us. Nearly every damn one of those codes that don't decode right are "Support" units…and the rest are probably just the screwups of our Intelligence folks…Hypothesis 'A', like I already described. Anyway, that's what we think." I concluded with a smile. "Uh…er…sir."

"Hmmm. Makes sense. Yeah, makes sense, damn it! You say you guys had 'a couple of hours' to put in on this?" He pulled open a drawer and lifted out a bottle of scotch. Spun the lid off, took a swig. Passed the bottle to me. "Have a hit," he offered. So I did. Choked a bit. Passed the bottle on down the row. The Captain continued. "Listen, gentlemen. I've been giving the Aggressor Code assignment for the last two and a half years, every nine-week cycle. You enlisted types get it as a volunteer extra-credit project, don't have to soil your hands with it if you don't want, but every cycle at least one group takes a stab at breaking the code. My officer classes get it as a for-credit assignment with three weeks to work on a solution, so every four-man team has to do their best with it. Counts for a lot of points on their final performance evaluation. You're going to see the Aggressor Code again, in a couple of big-ass, high-point exercises, so I suggest you fellows keep what you've worked out under your hats for now. Should give you an edge. I'm about 90% convinced you four bastards have got it right."

"Well thank you sir, but—"

"Wasn't finished. NO ONE has broken the Code yet. None of the enlisteds, none of the officers. As long as I've been at Holabird. As long as Holabird's been the Intelligence School, far as I know. That's been about fifteen years, I believe. I've seen plenty of piss-poor attempts, but they don't hold water, any of 'em. Not compared to this." He waved the printout of our solution around in the air. "Congratulations, gentlemen!" Like Sgt. Yoyo had, Captain Cameron stood, snapped to attention, saluted the four of us, Marine-style.

God-DAMN, but didn't *that* feel good!

Some few weeks later, along came one of those big-ass, high-point exercises the Captain had warned us about. It was called, charmingly, The Kill Board. Back in 1971 there was no such thing as desktop computers, or laptops, or iPads, or anything like that. Particularly as far as the Government was concerned. The Forest Service had been of the same institutional mindset as the Army: there was a big giant USFS mainframe computer back in Ft. Collins, Colorado, parked in a secure, air-conditioned room and attended by white-labcoated acolytes. You submitted jobs on punched cards, and in a few weeks got back a stack of printout if you were lucky. As far as the Forest Service Upper-Crust was concerned, this was the way computer science was going to go for the next two hundred years. Imagine their surprise when the technological tsunami of the PC Revolution washed over the agency about twelve years later.

Anyway, the Kill Board was what passed for an interactive video-game in 1971. There was a big segmented peg-board studded with several hundred cup hooks at the front of the room that the instructors sat behind. Hence the name...the second, 'Board' part. Bundles of little slips of paper hanging from the cup hooks. The players – that was us Ninety-Six Bravo trainees – occupied four-person tables out front. We were supposed to be simulating the intelligence staff of a Division-level Tactical Operations Center. Every twenty minutes or so, an instructor would call-up a runner from each team, and we'd get a handful of "dispatches" – some of those little slips of paper from off a hook on the no-peeking side of the Kill Board. The dispatches would describe action along the Division's combat front: enemy contacts, results of short-range patrols, radio intercepts, sightings of enemy movements, and the like. Our job was to make sense out of it. Once in every four hours, we submitted a status-report briefing document...what was called in the arcane jargon of military intelligence a SitRep – a Situation Report. To supplement the dispatches, we could "task" our surveillance resources: request patrols to certain map coordinates, ask for aerial reconnaissance overflights, grill imaginary prisoners for certain information...like that. If we struck on a viable source of data, back came another useful little paper slip and we'd have to make sense out of it. This exercise ran ten hours a day for three days, and was very intense.

Now, based on our degree of stupidity and ignorance, we succeeded in getting some of our own imaginary troops killed. There'd be an Aggressor artillery emplacement we hadn't spotted and warned Command about. Or a battalion-strength troop movement that had gone undetected, and our boys would unwittingly march right into it. Or a mysterious dug-in sniper unit that hosed-down one of our patrols with automatic weapons fire. A little slip of paper would come back saying, "Ambush at Grid Coordinates 99357:102110 by unanticipated sniper unit resulted in USMC casualties 12 KIA and 26 WIA. Nice work, you so-called Intelligence assholes!" The more of our own guys you got killed, the lower your score. Hence the name…the *first,* 'Kill' part.

Well, we had this one fictitious Aggressor buck-private that had been taken prisoner. We had him interrogated seven ways from Sunday. He told us his name was Izmir. He claimed to be a cook. He claimed to be assigned to the 155th Transport Company, and his convoy had been busted by a US airstrike while bringing hot chow up to his troops, and he'd been wandering aimlessly for three days, and he hadn't had any food or water, and he was only a draftee private who'd been a baker's assistant back home in Irkutsk, and he didn't know nothing about nothing. It was all a parcel of lies. According to the capture notes, his uniform tunic had stitchmarks where some insignia had been recently ripped off the shoulder, and from their shape it was inferred they might have been Aggressor Major's crescents. There was a military bank-deposit receipt in his shirt pocket that bore a six-digit number on it. Aggressor Code-Number! It decoded as 155th "Support" Brigade…making allowances for that screwed-up code business we'd labeled Hypothesis 'B'. Suggested to us it was one of those covered-up, duplicitous unit mission-descriptors! Everything else he said was either uncheckable, or a verifiable, outright lie, demonstrable by other intelligence that we already had in-hand. So we suspected Izmir was a secret, potential gold mine of information. Bust 'im with interrogation! We kept making up lists of questions for the Divisional MPs to grill him with, back at the PW lockup. We kept getting back lengthy notes on little slips of paper from behind the Kill Board. We kept devoting precious hours to trying to make Izmir's prattlings fit the tactical situation. It never fit. It never fit because it was invariably a parcel of lies.

Then Wes and I put our heads together. Came up with the $64,000 Question. Scribbled it on a request form and sent Monk up to the Kill Board to pose the query to the instructors:

Was P.W. named Izmir carrying any documents on his person when captured?

One of the instructors sent Monk to fetch us up for a private conference, and all four of us went dashing forward. *Sotto voce*, he told us "Yes. Izmir was carrying a folded-up map hidden in his boot. It's over there on the podium." He pointed us toward the lectern at the far right of the stage.

Lying flat-out on the lectern was a raggedly-torn and creased piece of topographic map. From the terrain, we instantly recognized a chunk of our Division's area of operations. There was a heavy red line marking a route from deep in Aggressor territory to a location immediately to our dug-in front, with a big red X. Symbols next to this line were recognizeable as Aggressor identifiers for Armored Infantry units, and an Aggressor code-number inside one of the boxes decoded as 244th Heavy Mechanized-Infantry Brigade. There was a timestamp, a bit smeared and blurry, that looked as if it read in Esperanto, "0415 *la dua Februaro*".

Today was *la unua Februaro*. Middle of the afternoon. Those rotten Circle-Trigon Bastards were planning a great big armored assault against our left flank for early tomorrow morning!

Well as you might imagine, our SitReps dwelt on this likely development for the balance of the exercise. Every further morsel of evidence from behind the Kill Board seemed to verify our urgent finding, in our minds. In response, Division moved men, equipment, and resources around and around. Every movement we made was met by lethal surprises from undetected Circle-Trigon baddies. Altogether, nine hundred and sixty of our guys got killed in the confusion, jumped by ambushes or picked-off by mortar barrages or blundered into unsuspected enemy positions. There was never any Armored assault. No one even saw any Aggressor tanks within twenty kilometers of the operations zone.

Following the conclusion of the Kill Board debacle, the instructional cadre debriefed us. The sergeant handling the debriefing had an inscrutable smile on his face when he got to the bit about Prisoner-of-War Izmir. "Twelve teams, gentlemen!

Twelve teams…and only two managed to ask the key question: whether this schmuck was carrying any intelligence-bearing documentation!" Members of the other ten teams emitted miserable groans. "He had a map, gentlemen! Here it is!" He brandished the topographic map with its heavy red line. More groans from ten out of twelve teams while the rest of us smirked. "Of the two teams that got to have a look at this map…too bad none of you eight morons bothered to turn it over!" He displayed the back side of the paper. There, neatly tabulated, was the answer to any Intelligence Analyst's dreams: units, schedules, missions, manpower strengths, weapons, locations of ammo and fuel dumps, coordinates, convoy movements, details on the fictitious counterintelligence ruse of a make-believe armored thrust on the US left flank …everything we could have needed to outfox that wily Aggressor. Izmir's name was shown as Major Izmir Kirchoff. Terse orders in Esperanto addressed him as a staffer of the Directorate of Field Intelligence, Sixth Combined-Arms-Army, operating within the Tactical Operations center of the 155th "Support" Brigade subordinate to CAA-6, Glorious Aggressor Nation, and ordered him to the front to transmit operations details tabulated hereon for the upcoming major infantry attack on the Cringing Yellow Capitalist Dogs. That would be us guys. We could have informed Division Command of all this stuff in a rip-roaring SitRep, and they would have had the Aggressor by the balls! It was our turn to groan in pain.

There's another bonehead mistake I vowed never in life to make again, literally or figuratively. Don't forget to turn things over and have a peek at the other side.

A week before our stint at Intelligence School concluded, my buddy Wes had night duty as assistant to the Officer of the Day. He got to pack a loaded, hip-holstered .45 automatic. He got to wear a nifty OOD shoulder insignia. He got to answer the telephone in crisp military fashion, from 6 p.m. until midnight. When he got off-duty, he sauntered through the darkened barracks and sat down on my footlocker, poked me quietly awake with his booted toe.

"What's up?" I asked sleepily. Around us, there was a lot of snoring. Wes waved me out onto the chilly balcony, and I shrugged into my field jacket and followed.

"Wull, I'm asittin there at the Top Sergeant's desk. Not snoopin or anything, y'know? There's this clipboard apeekin out from under a stack of magazines. Didn't have to pull it out, but there was this-here piece a paper. I could see two names typed on't. You'n me."

"Huh. What was it about?"

"Dunno for sure. But hand-scribbled down acrosst the bottom, that paper said, 'US Army Language School, Monterey, California'. Scribbled lahk someone's takin' notes from a phone call, y'know?"

Wow. That was a big one alright. Worth getting waked up over. "Anything else?"

"Yup. Then it said…'Germany'."

Woo-hoo! Army was going to ship the two of us off to Language School, teach us to speak, read and write German, then station us in Frankfurt or Munich or Berlin or something! Made sense – Wes and I were coming in at the top of the class. Tops by a mile, so a plum assignment seemed reasonable. What else could it mean? Germany! …The one in *Europe*! That was *heaps* better than Viet Nam! The two of us floated along on the elation of this intelligence until the very last day of our schooling, when we both received promotions to Specialist-Fourth-Class, along with travel orders stating our duty-station assignments. Speedy-Fours! Newly-minted Ninety-Six Bravos! Bound for the Language School and Germany! We zipped open the sealed, official-looking orders and gave them a read:

Destination: Long Binh Replacement Depot, Republic of South Viet Nam.

It ain't what a feller don't know that makes him a fool…it's what he knows that *ain't so*.

Henry Wheeler Shaw ("Josh Billings")

9

My Sorry Ass Gets Shipped to 'Nam

We took an Army shuttle-bus to the Baltimore Airport, Wes and I. He had no desire to face his ex-wife with the scars of that coldhearted breakup still festering, so he had decided to visit his widowed mom for a week. Then I prevailed on him to fly on out to the West Coast and take a few days R&R at the Family Compound. That peculiar establishment ought to prove interesting for him! I, on the other hand, was winging my way back to Elle, nonstop. She had been assuring me in her daily love-letter that Reddy missed me as much as she did...maybe more! In a week, we'd drive down to the Family Compound, if the geriatric Comet would make it that far. Speedy-Four pay was quite a bit more generous than buck-private, so in the back of my mind I had a scheme: retire the Comet to the car-crusher, and see what we could do about a new vehicle.

I got off the plane in Oregon with a measure of trepidation. Elle had not had much time to process that business about Long Binh. But, I told myself, both of us had expected all along that Viet Nam was my likely destination. Her dad had been in harm's way many times during his Air Force career. So had my dad. Didn't make it a whole lot easier. Worse still, I had no idea what the Army might intend to do with me in-country. A remote firebase on the DMZ? The big sprawling base at Cam Ranh Bay? A billet in Saigon? A festering hellhole in the Mekong Delta? We would have to just wait and see. I never imagined that the Army also had no idea what they might intend to do with me in-country, and wouldn't come up with an answer until I arrived at the Replacement Depot in Long Binh.

Those two weeks of leave were lovely. Early spring in Oregon, cool and showery, rhododendrons and daffodils blooming everywhere you looked. Early spring in the San Francisco Bay Area, coming on warm with dawn-to-dusk sunshine. When Wes came winging in to SFO, we toured him around the sights of San Francisco until his head spun with it. Then we buzzed him out to the East Bay suburbs, filled him with barbecue California-style, and good Napa Valley wines, and lit up a Hindenburg-sized bonfire in the enormous backyard firepit. Howled at the moon until three a.m.

Reddy, the perfidious traitor, fell deeply in love with my buddy Wes.

All too soon the leave was up. It was my dad who drove Wes and me to the Alameda Embarkation Station. Elle had tried to summon-up the pluck to do it herself, but she just had not been able to manage. She and I did our leavetaking back at the Family Compound. It was particularly teary…I don't think she truly believed I would be coming home except perhaps in a box. My mom did the best imitation of stiff-upper-lip I'd ever seen, but I could tell she was faking it. When my dad pulled through the parking lot in Alameda and dropped the two of us in front of those big doors, wearing Class-A uniforms and toting stuffed barracks-bags, it looked like he was going to lose it. He had gone up the ramp of a troopship bound for the Nazi-held shores of North Africa, thence the Middle East, once upon a time. When he headed out on deployment in 1942, I'm sure he was optimistic, and frankly, probably a little bit jazzed by the adventure he was embarking upon. I would never have admitted it at the time, but that's certainly the way I felt. But it was something else again, for him to send a son off into a war zone.

The cavernous Embarkation Station swallowed us whole. We had to surrender our Basic-Training issue. Olive-drab fatigues, fleece-lined field jackets, natty Class-A uniform…tossed ignominiously into vast bins. We were issued tropical fatigues, jungle camos, khaki uniforms for more formal wear. Surprisingly, the issuing civilians were upbeat and friendly…no one threw anything at our faces. Those accursed black combat boots with their insatiable appetite for shoe polish got swapped for lightweight, steel-soled, canvas-topped Viet Nam combat boots.

72

For evening wear, I guess, we got a nice pair of shiny, laced, black brogues, just in case we'd somehow come to love spit-polishing a goddamned set of footwear with Shinola every goddamned morning of our lives. New campaign-caps, new insignia, new olive-drab underwear, new olive-drab hankies. The rumor was, we weren't getting *white* hankies or t-shirts so it wouldn't be particularly easy to surrender to the Viet Cong by holding them up and waving, should we ever wish to. Well but that's just silly.

Nothing to do for four or five days but lay about. Write letters to Elle saying It's really boring here and I have no idea what's going to happen next. Mosey down to the mess hall three times a day for a fine, tasty, nourishing army-chow meal. Participate in policing-up cigarette butts. No one could figure out exactly who it was who had the gall to dump cigarette butts on the immaculate floors in there, but the Management was damned-certain going to keep that Facility *spotless!* That was another fun pastime: sweeping and waxing and buffing the five hundred acres of concrete floors in the vast Embarkation Station facility. Well okay…it wasn't quite *that* big. Three hundred fifty acres, tops.

Finally the day came around that they were ready for us. April twentieth, 1971. We formed up with proud Basic-Training precision, about a hundred of us, and marched to a set of big garage-type lift doors, singing a nice, raunchy Army marching song. Up the doors went with a theatrical flourish. Out into the weather…first time outside that giant human warehouse in a week. Charter buses waiting, idling. Stuff our barracks bags into the bins. Receive our order documents and our Permanent Records which, once again, we were warned to guard with our very lives and present intact to the administrators on the receiving end. I sometimes wondered what would happen to a GI who just stuffed his Permanent Record in a garbage can…would he cease to exist as far as the Army knew? Then the buses lumbered out, onto the Eastshore Freeway, north, then a trifle east, then out over the barren Vallejo hills, up across the Central Valley, across to their ultimate destination.

Travis Air Force Base. There, a big shiny jet aircraft waited for us, fueled and ready, pointed toward Viet Nam.

Now here was something interesting! This wasn't a military transport. A C-5 or a Hercules. It was a commercial jetliner. A stretch-DC-8 as I recall. With commercial symbols on its tail: TIA. Someone asked, and found out this stood for Trans-International Airways. I'd never heard of them. Of course I hadn't...it was evidently a commercial airline that had been acquired (or possibly *invented*!) by the Pentagon expressly for ferrying Army personnel from one place to another.

We clambered up the ramp while baggage-handlers schlepped our barracks bags into the cargo hold. Imagine my surprise when I was greeted at the top of the stairs by an attractive, uniformed, female Flight Attendant! It wasn't a military uniform, it was a Trans-International Airways uniform. And it fit her really well. "Welcome aboard, Sir!"she chirruped. As if (a) I were a *Sir*, and (b) I had any choice in the matter! It was 'festival seating'...find an empty chair and occupy it!...so Wes and I found seats together and strapped in. After a while, the engines fired up. The plane began to roll. It taxied endlessly. Was it going to *taxi* all the way to Viet Nam? Then someone gave the pilot the go-ahead, the Flight Attendants made their little speech about seatbelts and tray tables and flotation devices, and we were off!

First leg took us to Elmendorf Air Force Base in Alaska. Second leg took us to Haneda Air Force Base in Narita, Japan. Third leg took us down south over the China Sea, then over a forested coastline. "Have a look down, gentlemen," the pilot declared over the intercom. "That's Viet Nam!" I expected black puffs of antiaircraft fire, or bullet holes stitching through the metal of the wings. But nothing happened; we just kept on flying unmolested.

"Would you care for another cup of coffee, Sir?" our Flight Attendant chirruped. I guess she meant me.

As the TIA airliner descended for its landing at Bien Hoa Air Base, the perky Flight Attendants lined up on their stations for debarkation instructions. Who hasn't heard this, a thousand times?

"Please be certain your seat belt is fastened low and tight across your lap. Seat backs and tray tables must be in their upright and locked position. All carry-on items stowed in the overhead bins or under your seat." Then it got a bit surreal. "Oh, and if the aircraft comes under rocketfire or mortar attack while taxiing, put your head between your knees. As soon as the cabin doors are flung open, run like Hell." Words to that effect. Can't remember, exactly. When the plane's air-conditioning was turned off and the cabin doors flung open, the air temperature instantly rose to a hundred and five degrees. The relative humidity rose to a hundred and forty percent.

Buses awaited us on the tarmac. Ominously, their windows were covered with heavy wire mesh. The buses had no air conditioning. Whatsoever. In order to survive, all the windows had to be wide-open all the time. Naturally! So, the function of the mesh became apparent: to keep out thrown objects. Like hand grenades, for instance.

You see, all us newbies in-country were experiencing the same doleful thoughts: "What am I *doin'* here?? It's a *war zone*! Somethin's going to *happen*! And it's *not* going to be nice!

An open-topped jeep mounting a swiveling .50-cal machine gun swung into position ahead of the buses. A second gun-jeep took up trailing position. Stern-faced GI's grasped the guns' arming levers and jacked priming rounds into the chambers. This security measure comforted us newbies not in the least. The convoy rolled.

Ah, now, suddenly, *here* was our first glimpse of something a little bit more *positive* about this Viet Nam place! A couple of very cute Vietnamese girls, maybe eighteen years old, strutting along the roadside! They wore conical straw hats over cascades of thick black hair. Cool shades. Gold jewelry. Far more important, they both wore silken *ao dais.* If you are unfamiliar with the traditional feminine garb of Viet Nam, please *please* stop reading immediately and google-up a picture of a lovely Vietnamese woman wearing an *ao dai.* The outfit begins with demure, loose, pajama-like trousers of silk or rayon, generously-sized enough to fluff lightly on the breeze, unbelted but drawn tight at the waist, going right down to the elegant wearer's sandal-tops. These pantaloons are usually black, or white, but occasionally are executed in some other festive color. Then the top...oh, the top! The top can be any color, preferably light, brocaded solids but often riotous tropical prints. From the neck down, the top goes like this: snug, upright, narrow mandarin collar that cannot do anything except emphasize the slim, lengthy beauty of the wearer's neck. Bodice and sleeves tailored to fit figure-flattering tight-tight, right down to the wrists and down to the waistline at the spot where the wearer's luscious hips begin to gently broaden. Closure across one shoulder and down the side with neat little black-cord frogs. Then, oh then! The top flares down to a long, long skirt of diaphanous, floaty silk extending all the way to the wearer's ankles, a skirt which would be a snug silken sheath like a floorlength Hong Kong *cheongsam*, a skirt which would cover up those seductive silken pajama-bottom pants, *were it not slit on both sides, all the way up to the wearer's sweet sexy ass*! The skirt panels, fore and aft, swish about and float on the gentlest of zephyrs, and those two little, graceful, adorable young Vietnamese bonbons strolled along on their sandaled feet in their exotic *ao dais*, giggling to each other because a hundred newbie American GIs were getting what was likely to have been their first eyeful of the loveliest representatives of Asian womanhood on a very large, very populous continent.

Well that cheered us right up. We rather enjoyed the balance of the ride from Bien Hoa to Long Binh. Looked out the window at the passing sights. Green acreage of crops and paddy. Rustic, slummy little mud-walled villages. Big gray water-buffalo. Yardfuls of scrawny chickens. Marketplaces crammed with fresh provender, acrawl with shoppers. Small boys occupying rickety tables, selling what looked like two-liter bottles of strawberry soda-pop along the highway shoulder, but what we later discovered was gasoline...impromptu refueling stations for the zillions of 50cc Hondas that crowded the highway. It occurred to me later that those gas bottles would only need a rag stuffed down their necks to become a very unpleasant surprise when lit and hurled at a passing bus full of GIs, window-mesh notwithstanding. Anyway, the drive, like an instructive article on outlandish foreign lifestyles out of National Geographic, instantly turned into something quite different when we pulled through the main gate of the US Army Long Binh Replacement Depot.

The place was a *dump*!

The Long Binh camp was mostly two-story barracks buildings, with a few administrative structures scattered about. All the barracks looked the same. It appeared as if these quarters had been constructed back when the French colonial powers were operating Indochina as an enormous rubber plantation, a hundred and fifty years ago. Weathered clapboard siding, windows bare of glass or screen. Stairs and porches to the second story on each end, but sagging and paint-peeling in the blazing, broiling sunshine. Roofs of faded green, curling, asphalt tile. Not a scrap of landscaping. In fact, not a scrap of *anything* green and growing inside the entire rusty concertina-wire perimeter. Well…the stacked-up fabric sandbags which comprised the occasional machine-gun emplacement…*they* were green. I was amazed to find out that these tired, dreary barracks were less than five years old! They'd been constructed by US engineering contractors specifically for the Army Replacement-Depot function, but the merciless South Vietnamese sun and monsoon rains had aged them prematurely.

The camp stank badly. I discovered why, the moment my griping innards forced me to seek out a toilet. The 'facilities' were twelve-hole pit toilets without a trace of privacy. When I flipped up the seatcover, I found myself peering down into a very shallow hole. In fact, no hole at all, beyond the twelve or fifteen inches afforded by the wooden bench-seat. Pieces of newspaper had been placed on the concrete slab down in there! I was supposed to take position on the Seat of Ease and let 'er rip on top of that newspaper. A number of people had *already* had a go at my particular newspaper! No wonder the place stank so badly! But nothing like the way it stank at about two o'clock that afternoon when a crew of Vietnamese laborers came around, flipped-open a row of exterior trapdoors that accessed those newspapers below the thrones, and proceeded to dispose of the…er…um…human waste products by *piling the papers all up in a big heap, soaking the mess with gasoline, and lighting it on fire!* Gawd! Whoever heard of such a thing? What a sheltered existence I'd been leading for my first twenty-four years of flush-toilets and Pine-Sol!

I won't dwell on my six days in Long Binh. Mostly, I sat around tossing down copious drafts of water and sweating it right back out of every pore, certain that no human being could long exist in such a climate. It took me a few months to come to a peculiar realization: perhaps the Long Binh Replacement Depot was purposefully kept foul and horrid, so that if an individual got routed out to live in tents and holes in the ground in some stinkin' firebase on the DMZ, it would seem like a *step up*, luxury-wise, in comparison.

On my sixth day in the RepDep, I was called out of formation by name, along with twelve other people from my Fort Holabird Ninety-Six Bravo training cycle. They were going to send us in to Saigon, no more than fifteen miles west of Long Binh, as replacement analysts in a unit designated the 252nd 'Support' Company. 'Support', my ass! That designation was subterfuge for 'Military Intelligence'. We were no better than the godless Circle-Trigons!

One of our number had been set aside for other duties…redirected to a Tactical Operations Center for a line battalion 'way upcountry at Chu Lai. He was to be transported north by helicopter the afternoon of the following day. My good buddy Wes. I would not see him again for nearly a year.

10

The Parker Compound, Roast Beef, and Mai

Those of us destined for the 252ⁿᵈ "Support" Company climbed onto an olive-drab bus. We motored out the gates of the dismal Long Binh Replacement Depot, happy to see the backside of it. On up Highway 1A, the main-drag westward toward Saigon. The main-drag was suggestive of a U.S. Interstate, except for the traffic. Trucks, buses and cars, of course, but also growling, diesel-smoke-spewing Tank Retrievers and Construction Lowboys and Refueling Tankers. And ox-carts! Plodding along and lending a new definition to the term 'slow lane.' Little blue-and-yellow taxicabs, mostly Morris Minors. Public transport in the form of a three-wheeled scooter-like cab with a very small, open-air buslike affair welded on to the back…many, many of them. We were informed by the bus driver, an Old Saigon Hand, that these vehicles were called 'Lambros', since the scooter part was usually a modified low-displacement Lamborghini. "Check out the riders!" the bus driver clued us. Indeed, a Lambro could be crammed with anything ranging from eighteen miscellaneous Vietnamese citizens, to a 600-lb pig along with its swineherd, bound for market. In the small crevices between all these vehicles were a zillion 50cc Hondas. I counted no fewer than six passengers – poppa, momma, three assorted kids, and a babe in arms -- as well as perhaps fifty chickens, bound by their feet and slung over the handlebars, on one particular Honda. Such gross overloading was common, so this likely was far from a Guinness Record. Everyone was driving with their horns and their accelerators.

"Are there a lot of vehicle accidents?" I asked the driver.

"Hmp! *Lots* of 'em. It was the *French* taught 'em how to drive!" He laughed at his own wit. His eyes temporarily off the road, a couple of darting Hondas risked bloody death by changing lanes with five inches of clearance beyond our hurtling bus's front bumper. Our driver calmly stomped the brakes, blared the air-horn, and reaccelerated, all in a fluid, catlike motion. "Hit one of

them, fellas, and you'd better stop. Then back over him a few
times. Kill a slope, and you get a little reprimand. *Wound* one of
'em and you'll be supporting him and his family for life!"

First time – but not the last – I heard a citizen of South Viet
Nam, our loyal ally in time of war, called a 'slope'.

Our bus cruised on into the fringes of Saigon on 1A and we
had our first views of the sprawling capital. We approached the
snakey, mud-colored Saigon River. Slums lined both sides of the
watercourse. They appeared to be made out of millions of
flattened-out cans, Coca-Cola and low-end American beer-brands
prevailing, tacked onto slender wooden poles. Many were two-
story...a few seemed to stretch upward three stories. Lord knows
what the interior arrangements for floors, stairwells, plumbing,
cooking and ventilation were like. Some of these shanties
cantilevered out over the water. Something above two million
Vietnamese lived in primitive conditions like this, for Saigon had
grown from a drowsy tropical market-center of a couple hundred
thousand citizens in 1959 to over five million in 1971. Country
dwellers come to the capital, seeking economic opportunity...and
dubious safety from the peril of war.

The 1A crossed over the river into Saigon proper. The driver
made a sharp left across-traffic. Vehicles screeched and honked
and slid in various directions as the bus hurtled across the opposing
lanes. We made our way southward along beside the festering
slums.

"There she is, fellas! The Parker Compound. That bridge over
there is called Cau Binh Loi. Say it a few times so you can
remember it: 'Cow Bin Loy'! Means, "Binh Loi Bridge". Tell a
cabdriver that and he'll get you home, anywhere in Saigon."

The insouciant driver wheeled into the compound between
flanking guard stations, with only a peremptory wave of a pass
toward one of the four M16-toting gate-guards.

The Parker Compound had been a Thoroughbred Stables and
Riding-Academy, back in the French Colonial days. At the center
of the compound stood a stately two-story bungalow with clay-tile

roofs and mullioned windows, verandas on all four sides. Officer's quarters…administration…kitchen and mess-hall. There were several long godowns on the river-side. These had been stables for the riding stock, but now were barracks for enlisted men. That is not to say we EMs had to sleep on old hay-bales and decades of compacted horse-crap. The stables had been cleaned up and renovated, to a degree. The floors were poured concrete now, the lockers, chairs, tables, and bunks were the Army's Very Best, and the retrofit restrooms, thank the Benevolent Almighty, were *not* Long Binh shit-burners. Flush toilets and hot showers. Don't drink the water, we were warned.

We were made welcome and fed lunch. Roast beef. A tour of the compound revealed it to be no bigger than about three acres, but snug and self-contained. There was a pretty nice club in one tin-roofed building, with a nice polished-wood bar, stuffed chairs, muted lighting, big stereo tapedeck and lots of 'Sixties and early-'Seventies pop groups prevailing: Creedence, CSN&Y, Doors, The Who, BeeGees, Beatles, Dylan…like that. A sign advised us that mixed drinks were twenty-five cents, beer was fifteen, a can of coke for a dime. Pretty reasonable! We were permitted to take the afternoon off to get our gear cleaned up and stowed away, and rest up from our travels. In the morning, we'd have some work details to do. Don't worry, it won't be too backbreaking. We'd be shipped over to the Intelligence duty-stations, maybe in a couple of weeks. This all seemed suspiciously casual and laid-back to my cynical ear.

I encountered an odd surprise as I trudged across the broad concrete floor of the barracks, bound for the cot I'd been assigned. I nearly stepped on a slowly-moving creature on the floor, dusty from having traveled a long way under furniture and across dusty yards. A *rat*? A gigantic bug of some kind? No…it was a *fish*! The critter was slowly flopping its way across the concrete, using its pectoral fins in a clumsy imitation of walking on legs. "Jesus!" I hollered. "A fish!"

One GI, sprawled on his rack, looked up from a comic book that seemed to be holding his interest. "Walking Catfish," he informed me. He was the only guy in the barracks who seemed to have any particular reaction to this wildlife phenomenon. A wizened Vietnamese woman who'd been sweeping-up far across the barracks threw down her broom and dustpan, grabbed a banged-up No. 10 tin, and scurried over. She deftly plopped the Walking Catfish into the can. "Dinner for Honorable Baby-sans," the comic-book aficionado opined, egregiously mixing-up numerous arrogant racial stereotypes. "Those fish come up out of the river sometimes." Well here I was, Toto…not in Kansas anymore. For sure!

The Parker Compound, home to the 252nd "Support" Company and no one else, was situated about two miles away from Tan Son Nhut Airbase and the Military Assistance Command Viet Nam (MACV) headquarters compound. It was one of a network of small compounds, Bachelor-Officer Quarters, and other US Personnel living arrangements scattered around town. During the Tet Offensive of 1968, the North Vietnamese Army and Viet Cong had swarmed into Saigon in large numbers. There had been loss of US lives in these widely-strewn facilities, but it could have been a lot worse. NVA units had assembled in Company- and Battalion-strength, just across the river. They had marched – Marched! In formation! Like a Moscow May-Day Parade! – across the Binh Loi Bridge while the Parker Compound residents hunkered-down behind sandbags, refraining from firing a shot or making a squeak. Live and let live, the NVA had evidently decided. Since 1968, only two years before, the Army had made the decision to concentrate personnel in the MACV Compound, and little-by-little they were closing down the farther-out ancillary quarters. Parker Compound was due to be abandoned within the next four weeks. Us newbies were going to be the closing-down crew and the labor force for schlepping everything on down to MACV.

So for a couple weeks we tidied-up. Here's where the Army's infinite wisdom manifested itself, in a fashion that illustrated the oxymoronic value of the term 'military intelligence'. Just prior to abandonment, the Parker Compound would undergo a complete inspection. The 252nd brass would take the resulting scores right on their Permanent Records. Brass, I discovered, tended to live in dread of the minions of the Inspector General's office.

Hmpf…Inspector-General! I had visions of Walter Slezak driving a gypsy cart onto the Parker Compound, and Danny Kaye in a glitzed-up Balkan military officer's uniform and a monocle, conducting the inspection. I considered warning the Commanding Officer not to forget that the pellet with the poison was in the flagon with the dragon, but the chalice from the palace held the brew that was true. Anyway, it occurred to me before I'd embarrassed myself that the bit was from The Court Jester, not The Inspector General. And there were no guarantees the CO would be familiar with old Danny Kaye musical comedies. Or have a particularly quixotic sense of humor. Or any sense of humor at all. So I bent my back to fill sandbags, paint corrugated-tin walls, and generally spruce-up the place we were all set to abandon. The days were blazing-hot and the humidity there along the Saigon River was two-hundred-and-eighty percent, but we got to work in t-shirts. Or bare-skinned, if we wished. And we got all the roast beef we could eat.

Roast beef was a contentious point at the Parker Compound. Evidently, one of the mess sergeants had pissed-off someone up the supply chain. I believe the divided loyalties of a Vietnamese girlfriend were involved. We'd been put on a special, secret shit-list to receive *nothing but* beef-roasts for lunch and dinner entrees. Forever, apparently. On the afternoon we arrived, it had been going on for eighty days straight! Since much of the personnel lunched and dined elsewhere, at mess halls nearer their duty stations, things had proceeded just a little bit short of Armed Rebellion. But the Compound cadre was getting damned tired of roast beef. Fortunately, I rather liked a nice medium-rare slice of RB, with a little hot horseradish (plenty of *that* on-hand!) so it didn't matter very much to me. In a couple weeks the Torture by Beef-Roast would be a thing of the past anyway, when we began to dine at the MACV Compound's Thousand-Man Mess. Catchy name for a restaurant, don't you think?

Somewhere around the beginning of May 1971, the General Inspection over and passed swimmingly, I donned crisp, clean Lightweight Tropical Fatigues and natty VN Jungle boots, and hopped on a truck bound for MACV. It was time to report for intelligence duty!

I had been assigned to a pretty prestigious outfit. This was an intelligence center that served the toplevel needs in that respect for all Allied forces in Viet Nam. Participation was evenly-spread between US Army, Marine Corps, Navy, Air Force, and our counterparts in the military branches of South Viet Nam. The Center was called a "Joint" operation because of this. I will just call my duty assignment the "Joint Intelligence Command" or "Joint Command" in order to do a weak job of preserving the Center's quasi-classified identity, although I'm pretty sure such a caution is unnecessary after all these years.

Joint Command was housed in a windowless one-story building. It was perhaps the size of a large Oregon department store, like a BestBuy maybe, or a Safeway, and was of just about the same construction: tipped-up concrete panels on a concrete-slab foundation joined with cast-in-place pillars. Steel roof over metal girders. Suspended false ceilings of sound-absorbent panels, and fluorescent lighting. The interior was divided into several large bays, but there were also dozens of smaller rooms given over to specialized tasks. A great big mainframe computer lived in a central room, guarded by tight security. Because of this computer, the building was air-conditioned...one of the very few US Army facilities in Saigon to enjoy this luxury.

The Joint Command building was well-guarded on its external perimeter. Access was through a single gate, manned 24-hours by a squad of well-armed, very alert Vietnamese Army troops. Any vehicle entering was subject to careful inspection, including undercarriage, scanned by mirrors, or occasionally by a fellow sliding right under on a mechanic's crawler. Around the high perimeter wall, which was of masonry topped by rolls of barbed wire, very decorative and attractive, there were half a dozen towers with two guards in each, and a sinister-looking M60 machine gun. Altogether, a festive ambience, not unlike a nice maximum-security penal institution. All personnel had to display an I.D. badge at all times: when entering, on-site, or leaving. As well as

US and VN military staffers, there were a few short-term visitors from other involved nationalities. There were civilian maintenance workers and canteen staff and cleaning-ladies, all Vietnamese. And there were clerical staff: stenographers, computer operators, and typists. Every one of these civilian employees had their bags, pockets, purses, and occasionally their persons inspected, entering and leaving. One afternoon, a very humble cleaning-lady was detained because she was carrying home a bouquet of flowers she'd picked on the premises, their stems wrapped in a moistened TOP-SECRET document! At the end of the day the civilian employees walked from the front door, through the security checkpoint, and down the lane to Nguyen Van Troi street to catch buses or taxis. Rain or shine. We US troops had the luxury of jumping on an Army bus right outside the doors, and zipping through security en masse, airily waving our I.D. cards. A bit of *arrogance*, there? Alternately, a few of us could buddy-up in one of the 252nd Company jeeps or deuce-and-a-halfs, and motor ourselves on back to our quarters.

On my first day, I was shown around the facility by one of the Old Hands, a fellow who'd been in-country for three whole months. Photo-interpretation lab. Computer facility. Message center. Intelligence archive. Order-of-Battle shop. Various smaller rooms dedicated to arcane tasks. A few unlabelled doors with crypto-locks, for which I would never know exactly what went on inside. The lunch-counter canteen was pointed out, just out the door and across the inner courtyard...I was free to buy snacks there at break times, or have a light lunch there, although most Army analysts preferred to zip across Nguyen Van Troi street to the Third Field Hospital's very fine mess-hall for lunch. Once in a while, Third Field's dining-room's admitting NCO would sniff out that we were not Hospital personnel and turn us away, but the good chow was worth the minor risk. One of the fellows who'd recently packed up and gotten on a plane for home had made me the gift of a pair of bandage scissors. Stick them in the pencil-pocket of my fatigue shirt and I'd easily pass for a medic...the scissors trick would get me into Third Field's mess hall every time! I never got nabbed by a panicked nurse as I walked Third

Field's hallway to perform an emergency corpsman-type tracheotomy with those scissors on a rush-rush bloody mess of an admission, and I don't know what I would have done if I had been. The other advantages of going across the street were (1) getting out of the dratted Joint Command building for half an hour or so, and (2) the chance of hobnobbing with a genuine American Female Nurse, if your luck was off-the-scale good. The disadvantage was that the insane traffic on Nguyen Van Troi was an excellent, high-probability way of getting yourself killed.

After the Joint Command introductory tour, I and two other new-guys were shunted back to Order-of-Battle. In this big bullpen, data from all four Military Regions of the country were catalogued and analyzed. I was briefed on the two tasks I would perform for the ensuing year. First of these was sifting through the morning reports for what was termed "enemy-initiated incidents" for MR-I and MR-II. Like for example:

Ban Me Thuot 5/15/71 0530local: Unidentified enemy threw hand-grenade into People's Guard compound. Result 0 kia, 1 wia, 3 M16 destroyed.

This data was codified and summarized, and made up part of the daily SitRep that went on up the line to Command. Boring stuff, huh? It occasionally added up into meaningful patterns.

The second of my duties was with the "Edit" element. There were four of us. Spec-4 Ernie Marsden, who'd gone through Ninety-Six Bravo training with me at Fort Holabird. An E-7 Sergeant named Timmons – no one to my knowledge ever used his first name, and it's even possible he did not have one. A Spec-5, Bobby Sanders, who was about six weeks short of finishing up his tour and heading back to the Land of the Big Supermarket. And me. We were supposed to put together the daily SitRep, type it up, make it pretty for the Command brass. Once a week, there was an Intelligence Extract...a summary of the week's events. Once a month, the OB section put together an OpRep – Operations Report – that might run to ten or fifteen pages. The OpRep contained OB staff conclusions about what all the little tidbits might mean, what trends were observeable or shaping up, where the near future might lead. Aha, now *this* was actual intelligence analysis! Unfortunately, all the Edit boys were supposed to do was type it up. We were expressly warned-off of particularly trying to exercise our brains. Or our Ninety-Six Bravo training.

We also had a bunch of other typing jobs thrust upon us. Awards citations were one of these jobs. What a pain in the ass! Since the various branches of the Intelligence apparatus were pretty rear-echelon functions, and since the War was kind-of winding down in 1971, what with Kissinger trying to find a face-preserving way out for us in those talks going on in Paris, there seemed to be lots of extra time and energy for the line officers to devote to putting up their guys for medals and awards. If you've never been in the Service, you've got to understand this: a unit whose personnel garnered lots of awards carried high prestige in the eyes of the Brass on up the line. A unit that carried high prestige was good for the careers of the junior officers in that unit. Junior officers were the ones responsible for putting up the enlisted personnel for awards. Hmmm…can you see the conflict of interest here? Well, consequently, lots of Joint Command Speedy-fours and Speedy-fives were awarded Joint Service Commendation Medals. Or Bronze Stars. *Silver* Stars, even. With oak-leaf clusters! Often, as a going-home attaboy congratulations at the end of a routine tour of duty. Often, for little more than keeping their desks tidy. Guys out in the jungle might get their legs blown off at the knees under heroic circumstances and not wind up with a Silver Star. Us Edit specialists had to type up the awards citations for our own *hors de combat* units. Yeah, it made you a little cynical after a while.

I'd always liked pounding on a typewriter. I could hammer out about 55 wpm. We had a nice IBM Selectric. We did NOT have word-processing, spell-checking, digital save/recall/edit, find/replace function, cut/copy/paste, format, auto-columnize…none of that *existed* in 1971. So one had to fix errors with an ink-eraser, or just rip out a screwed-up citation and type it over again. Colonel Childers, the commanding officer of the OB element, insisted that all his correspondence be *letter-perfect*. I don't think this was a particular crotchet on his part...rather, Business As Usual in the Army. No errors, no misspellings, no strikeovers, no erasures. Many's the time I'd get all the way down to the signature-block without misadventure on one of Col. Childers' letters, and then type "Sincerly Yurs," DAMN!!! Nothing to be done for it. That totally-screwed letter would get ripped off the platen, crumpled into a lethally-tight ball, and hurled viciously against the nearest wall, with an obscene comment or two as if obviously the typewriter were at fault. Then after I calmed down, I'd start over with a fresh blank piece of paper.

So we had a couple of the OB branch's secretaries to occasionally help with the typing. Thi Thich Lon was a nice, attractive middle-aged married lady who spoke pretty good English. She was pretty busy most of the time, and tended to rule the roost as the most-senior secretary. She could sometimes be prevailed on to help out the Edit boys in a pinch, with our typing needs. The other one, Ngo Minh Nu, was a little less cooperative, usually...she had three kids at home. And she was five months pregnant. That omygod-I-can't-believe-I-swallowed-an-entire-volleyball stage of pregnancy – and she was a teeny tiny little Asian woman to begin with when *not* pregnant. That, plus the responsibilities of motherhood, had gone down hard with her...judging by the photographs on her desk, in her younger years she was pretty glamorous. She was not bearing the processes of motherliness with what you'd call serenity. It came out as a mild case of snappishness and a reluctance to be particularly helpful when asked. So in the first week I worked in OB/Edit, Colonel Childers promised the Edit guys he'd see if he could get us our own personal, exclusive, non-shared typist.

I liked Thi Thich Lon quite a bit. She was friendly, and actually sort of motherly toward me. I was only twenty-four, after all, and probably looked about seventeen. She kept asking me questions about myself, and when I stuck a nice framed photo of Elle on my desk, she had to know every last little detail about that whole business. Your *wife*?? You aren't old enough to have a wife, are you? You just a little boy! You got any babies yet? You know how do that? You got any questions about making babies, you just ask Auntie Lon! You send her money, that pretty lady? She have to work? Where she live? She live with your parents? You write her every day? How you meet her...how you get her to marry you, pretty lady like that? It was kind of touching. All the American staff called her "Lon"...it was her first name, after all, since the Vietnamese tradition had it that your "given" name came last and your "family" name came first. The form of address just seemed a little too familiar and vaguely disrespectful to me. They called the other secretary "Nu." When I listened to how the Vietnamese military personnel addressed the ladies, they would say 'ban Lon'...the other secretary was 'ban Nu.' I guessed that the prefix implied "married-lady." Unmarried women were addressed with the honorific 'cô,' at least in *South* Viet Nam. So I Americanized this a little bit, and started calling the two of them 'Mrs. Lon' and 'Mrs. Nu.' It sort of caught on in the OB shop, and in a while everyone else was using these forms of address. To me, it just felt a tiny bit more respectful. I tuned-up my ear for precision Vietnamese, and came to discover these two names were more closely approximated as "*ban Lun*" and "*ban Nya*," spelling notwithstanding.

One morning about three weeks after I started working at Joint Command, I wandered through the OB bay intending to slide unnoticed into the Edit workroom at about ten after eight...the bus from the Parker Compound had been a little late. Sgt. Timmons was standing in the doorway glancing worriedly at something inside the very cramped Edit shop. He looked a bit troubled. Marsden and Sanders sprawled in a pair of chairs out in the hallway drinking foul-tasting OB coffee.

"What's up, Sarge?" I asked Timmons.

"Looks like we got us our new typist." He jerked his thumb in an unviewable direction around the doorjamb toward the inside of the Edit room. I leaned past him and peered around the doorframe.

In an uncomfortable metal folding chair sat a small woman dressed in a flowery *ao dai*. My first impression was, "My goodness, that's a lovely-looking young lady!" She may have looked lovely, but she also looked scared to death. "What's her name?" I asked the sergeant.

He examined some papers clutched in his hand. "Tuoi Mai," he pronounced carefully, trying to get it right. I don't think his Vietnamese was very good, but I was not one to talk, having not a single word of Viet at my command.

It occurred to me that I ought to greet my new co-worker. It was on my tongue to say "Hi, Mai!" but that sounded outrageously flippant. And having those two syllables rhyme, as appropriate with the Vietnamese 'ai' diphthong, just made matters worse. Instead, I stepped inside the door and said, "Good morning, Miss Mai."

She was Miss Mai from that moment forward, to all the other American staff, as long as she came to the Edit shop. The others picked up on it right away. She was Miss Mai in my mind from that moment on. And in my heart.

11
I Have a Few Words with Miss Mai

D oes she speak much English?" I asked Timmons. The girl had hardly reacted to my attempt at greeting her.

"Don't think so."

"Well do you suppose she speaks French?" It was not uncommon for many Viet citizens over about age forty to speak fairly fluent French. Quite a few younger ones as well. A holdover from decades of French colonial exploitation. Escaping the poverty and uncertainty of Viet Nam by emigrating to Paris was the dream of many Vietnamese youth. Tens of thousands had managed to do it.

"Lord, I don't know!" the sergeant said. "Do *you* speak French?"

In fact, I was fairly fluent. "*Un peu*," I told the sarge. He made a go-ahead-and-give-it-a-try gesture with the palm of his hand.

"*Excusez-moi, mademoiselle*," I tried gently. "*Bon matin. Comment ça va, s'il vous plaît? Est-ce que vous parlez peut-être la langue Français, Mademoiselle Mai?*"

Miss Mai's eyes grew as big as saucers. But she timidly shook her head No.

"Nope, no French," I reported. "Do you think maybe she speaks any Russian?"

The sarge choked out my name. "Christ on a crutch, Speedy...do you speak *RUSSIAN*??"

"*Malo*," I said, "...*tozhe, nye ochen harascho.*" All right...I was showing off a little. I had to derive *some* benefit from that horrible semester!

"Russian! Lordalmighty! Well okay, give it a go."

Again I approached her. "*Dobriy dyen...kak dyela? Pojal'sta, genschina...vwi gavaritye poRusski, da?*"

Miss Mai's eyes seemed to come out on stalks. For the first time, she smiled tentatively. Again, the little shake of the head.

Damn! That exhausted my limited language skills. I wasn't

going to try Aggressor on her…Esperanto, I should say. And I spoke not one single syllable of Vietnamese. *"Nyet…Nyetu!* Nope, no Russian either," I reported.

But it didn't matter. The girl had realized I was attempting to communicate with her. It was more than, or at least different from, what all the scary, big, smelly, loud, gruff American uniformed strangers had done for her so far in the last couple days throughout her hiring process, which amounted to trying to get her to understand English by repeating things louder, more often, and more insistently. The intentions of my attempt had gotten through to her if the words had not. We'd begun to form a bond, she and I, based on communication. The bond would grow and blossom into something else. I gave her an encouraging smile. And she returned the favor, did the lovely, shy little Miss Mai.

One of the first things I searched-out about Miss Mai that first morning was how to spell her name. And how to say it properly. I fetched one of the OB department's English/Viet dictionaries to do a little research. Vietnamese is a difficult language for the English-speaking tongue. When you see it written, it doesn't look so tough. Every word is only one syllable long, more or less. Some of them look like two syllables…for example, the universally most-common Vietnamese name *ever*: **Nguyen**. Must mean "Smith" or "Jones" in translation. Looks like two syllables, right? But no…it's pronounced like '**nwin**' -- only one syllable. Anyway, that's the way it seemed to me. I didn't get any official training or tutoring in spoken Vietnamese or anything like that. The Army had wasted not so much as thirty seconds' training-time in giving us any orientation on Vietnamese language, customs, culture or history. Not so much as a 3x5-card "Helpful Phrases for the Saigon-Bound GI" cheat-sheet. Neither I nor any of my classmates were prepared to say "please", "thank you", "My name is Specialist Such-and-such," or "Where's the bathroom?" Not even "Gimme a beer" or "How about a kiss, sweetie?" or "Stick up your hands and surrender or I'll shoot!" In retrospect, it was stupid and arrogant of me not to seek out some of this knowledge on my own, before I was flown eight thousand miles to an exotic distant country for a solid year. I regret it profoundly.

Where written Vietnamese got tricky was on all the zillions of little diacritical marks over and under the vowels, many of which dictated the tonality of the word: high, low, rising, falling, and so forth. The marks are impossible to reproduce on most typewriters (except probably those in Hanoi or Saigon!), and somewhere between difficult and impossible on most computer word-processing software. Well, Miss Mai didn't usually write her name very much, and when she did, she just scribbled it off like everyone does. But it appeared as if her name, formally, would have been written:

Tuôi Mãi

That's the way it appeared on her official Joint Command I.D. tag, if you looked very closely – a couple of wiggly marks that meant a lot, hovering over each of those two vowels.

I couldn't discover if Vietnamese proper names had meanings that were the same as if these words were used in everyday conversation, but if one pokes around in an English/VN dictionary, her family name may very well translate as "fresh" or "bright"…something like that. And her given name translates as "tomorrow", or, if spoken reduplicatively as "Mãi-Mãi", frequently the case in many Asian languages when speaking someone's name familiarly or affectionately, the meaning changes to "forever". So if my weak attempt to ferret-out an English meaning for her name was anywhere near the mark, she was Miss Fresh-Tomorrow, or perhaps Miss Bright-Forever. A lot of metaphorical high-optimism for a single small, shy, pretty girl to carry on her slim shoulders. But I liked it. I liked it a lot.

Well, that first morning Miss Mai appeared, we decided we ought to get right down to work. I had a stack of teletype flimsies to wade through. Timmons had a couple of SitReps that needed typing-up. He got Miss Mai settled at the Selectric, issued her a stack of erasable-bond, and flooped-down the rough drafts in front of her. No further instructions were required. No further

93

instructions were *possible*, given the language gap. Miss Mai rolled a blank sheet into the platen and lined things up.

Then she did a rather peculiar thing. She cracked her knuckles, every one of them, both hands. The entire Edit element stopped what we were doing and gawped. She smiled shyly. Then she put one slim hand on her chin, another on her opposite temple, and exerted torsional pressure. And she cracked her cervical vertebrae, every one. Clik-clik-clik-clik-clik-clik! C1 to C7 in precise order. Atlas right on down to the vertebra prominens. Audibly, from clear across the room. Twice! Leftward-twist, then rightward.

Turns out, this was Miss Mai's loosen-up ritual before commencing typing. Every day, morning and afternoon. Oh well, different countries different customs. Her fingers were slim, feminine and elegant, with dainty knuckles, and her neck was pretty nice too...so, no harm being done. Well, whatever! Soon, she was rattling away on the keys, and I turned my attention back to the miscellaneous Enemy-Initiated Incidents to be found within that pile of flimsies on my desk.

I was pretty deep in concentration when I received a jolt of electricity just above the collar of my fatigue shirt and right into the tissues of the back of my neck. It was Miss Mai...she had touched me very lightly with two of her fingertips to get my attention. This was my first experience with the phenomenon of ectoplasmic psychical energy-discharge that she seemed to impart to me on the infrequent occasions we made any sort of skin-to-skin contact...an attention-getting touch or an accidental graze of bare hand-backs. I spent many long hours wondering what that was all about. Eventually I surreptitiously asked around a little bit, but no one else confessed to having experienced her ability to zap with her fingertips. Maybe it was all in my head. Anyway, she'd finished the SitRep and evidently was wondering whether it was typed-up all right. She proffered the typescript for my approval.

"All done, Miss Mai?" I asked.

She shook her head No. Pointed to her I.D. badge. Underlined the name "Mai" with her finger. "Mai," she said firmly. Okay, I got it. Mai was just fine between us two. I'd save the Miss-Mai for when anyone else was in earshot.

Then she very gently touched the camo-green nametag stitched above my shirt pocket. The psychoelectric discharge didn't stop my heart, but it gave it a pretty good defibrillatory thrill. Interesting to know the phenomenon didn't hesitate to pass right through cotton cloth. She underlined my last name with her fingernail, and raised her eyebrows quizzically. Oh…I get it. What's *my* given name! "My name?" I asked. She nodded uh-huh…said "name" very distinctly. Her diction was low and musical, like a kitten purring. It was our first lesson in English. The first of many. So I told her my name. Wrote it out for her on a scrap of paper.

I must say, she got it *all wrong*. Five letters. Two stinkin' syllables. No tricky diphthongs or anything. She got the accent on the wrong syllable and she messed up both vowels. But the way she said my name was so ditzy and endearing, it rendered me breathless. I wouldn't have corrected her for the world. She rehearsed it three or four times, getting it spectacularly wrong each time. That's what she called me forever after. By common agreement, secretly arrived-at by god-knows-what unspoken *sub rosa* pact, she used the short name only between the two of us when no one else was in earshot.

Sergeant Timmons brought Miss Mai another handful of letters to type and I went back to my OB flimsies. Strangely, I had a difficult time concentrating for the rest of the morning.

A couple days after Miss Mai started working for us, waiting in the Edit in-box first thing in the morning was a draft of a letter to be sent out over Colonel Childers' signature. I had arrived at my usual 7:45, but our shiny-new typist had a starting time of 8:00, determined by the arrival time of the city bus she rode every morning. Master-Sergeant Thompson stuck his head around the corner. "Get right on that letter, will you, Specialist? Needs the CO's signature and then into the messenger pouch before 10:30."

I gave him the "OK" sign.

"Letter-perfect!"

He did not need to remind me. I cranked a sheet of bond into the Selectric. Started rattling away. Two paragraphs of officialese. Got down to the signature block. Typed, "Sincerely Yours, Colomel Wm. Childers, CO, Jt Cmd OB Saigon, VN" When I ratcheted the completed letter off the platen, the misspelling of Childers' rank leaped off the page and bit me on the nose. "Damn it!" I yelled. Wadded up the letter and threw it against the nearest wall.

By 8:02, there were six more paper-wads at the foot of that goddamned wall. It was getting so I couldn't type the goddamned *date* without committing some kind of typo. And then Miss Mai glided in. Took a look at the situation. Made an instantaneous assessment, correct in all respects. "I do it!" she told me. I was so damned frustrated by that point I conceded the Selectric to her, willingly.

As I turned my attention to less stressful matters, specifically, the horde of snipings, grenade attacks, booby-trap deployments, rocketings, mortar fire, machine-gun bursts and so forth that had been Enemy-Initiated in Military Regions I and II over the last twenty-four hours, Mai got to typing. She'd been thoroughly briefed on the meaning of "letter-perfect" – no errors, no misspellings, no strikeovers, no erasures. Her complete lack of familiarity with English was actually beneficial to her typing skills. With a detached ear I listened to the rattle of the Selectric's type-ball as she dashed through the Colonel's letter.

The typing stopped. Mai was looking intently at the page, gnawing on a corner of her lip. "Tch!" she said, very softly. Ripped the paper off the platen. Wadded it into a tight ball. Tossed it – rather a bit too gently, by my lights – against the wall. Rolled in a new page and started over.

It took her four tries, but she finally got to the signature block. Got it typed with no hesitation. Smiled happily to herself, unaware I was surreptitiously watching. She rolled the letter out and brought it over to me for my approval. Not that this was our protocol, particularly. I wasn't her supervisor or anything. Colonel Childers read over his own correspondence and would have made any shortcoming clear...in rather a clement, avuncular tone, actually -- he was a pretty nice CO. Miss Mai stood by while I gave it a scan, bouncing ever so slightly on her toes.

"Um," I said. I hadn't meant to be heard. But Miss Mai reached past my shoulder and grabbed my red pencil out of the pencil-cup. She handed it to me with a little smile of rue and surrender. In the salutation, she had typed, "Der Sirs:" I stuck a caret in the appropriate place where there needed to be an 'a'. Mai said, very softly, "Tch!" And went back to try again.

When she said "Tch!" four more times and hurled four more balls of paper against the wall, my heart was breaking for her. "Mai," I begged. "You take a rest. Have some tea. Let me try once." I put a restraining hand on top of the piled-up Erasable Bond and waved her out of the chair.

"I do it!" she insisted, more forcefully that I believed her capable. She refused to vacate. "I do!" Defeated, I left her to it.

After six more attempts and six more utterances of her little "Tch" of frustration and six more paperwad projectiles, she believed she had it. Letter-perfect. She slid the final product in front of me. I gave it a very careful read. Yep…letter-perfect. "Good work, Mai!" I congratulated her.

Lingeringly, Mai kissed the tip of her index finger. Then she touched the kissed finger to the back of my hand. I received the usual zap of cosmic charge. Her fleeting smile was not so much one of self-congratulation as it was of gratitude. But I barely noticed. I was still dealing with that finger-kiss.

12

My Experiences at Joint Command

It seemed as if I and my cronies were always on the lookout for ways to get out of the Joint Command building. The truth was, my OB "Enemy-Initiated Incidents" duties took about forty-five minutes to polish off, max. Editing tasks were up-and-down, depending on what wound up in the in-box, but rarely comprised more than an hour or two at the worst. With my shiny-new typist, the Edit stuff went a lot faster than at first. My duty-day, however, ran from quarter-to-eight in the morning to five-forty-five p.m. Ten hours to fill up. Risking my neck to get across the boulevard to Third Field Hospital for lunch was good for maybe an hour. We were not punching any timeclock. As long as there was no flagrant abuse to attendance requirements, no one checked on departure and arrival times. Alternately to Third Field, there was another enlisted-personnel mess about a mile away…a good stroll down the road-shoulder if you didn't get whacked by the side-view mirror of a speeding bus. Or, this other mess could be reached by a rip-roaring five-minute jeep ride, if any jeep was parked out-front unattended. Lunching there was good for an hour and a quarter…but the chow was not so great. Then too, early in the day someone would have to go over to the South Vietnamese Headquarters Compound to retrieve the message flimsies. You'd have to check out an M16 and a few magazines for security's sake – you'd be transporting classified documents, f'Chrissakes! **SECRET** at least, or maybe **TOP SECRET**! Take a jeep, zing out the gate, turn immediately left, then left again. The SVHC was right next door! Their front-gate security measures were pretty rigorous, mainly because it was almost entirely a Vietnamese military operation and us American GIs were "foreign nationals." So we came under very close scrutiny…reverse nationalistic jingoism that you just had to put up with. Once inside, you went around to the back of a big building dubbed the "Vietnamese Pentagon" – yeah, in your *dreams,* Nguyen! The back door seemed like the servant's entrance. Just inside was the

Communications Office. They always had the flimsies packed up and ready in a big canvas bag, with a wire twistie through the zipper for security's sake. This was a two-man duty…someone had to stay outside with the jeep, or it would surely disappear.

Another escape from the confines of Joint Command was a jaunt over to the Base Exchange at Tan Son Nhut. Us junior enlisted personnel could always come up with some necessary item or another we just *had* to buy, and anytime after completion of our no-sweat "intelligence" duties one of our two Command Sergeants could be counted on to cough up a set of jeep-keys for a BX run. Heck, half the time he'd come with us! Packed six or eight to a jeep, we'd make the short run over to Tan Son Nhut. Kill an hour or so, wandering the Exchange aisles and making a leisurely jeep-cruise down the palm-lined boulevards on the way back from the big airbase.

Our little fleet of jeeps required constant, careful maintenance. This would positively require a jaunt out to the Battalion compound. This was a ramshackle camp all the way around at the far side of the Tan Son Nhut runway! Never any shortage of volunteers to take one of the jeeps out for an oil change and a tire check! In 1971, Tan Son Nhut Airbase was both a military airfield and Saigon's main commercial airport. It had a *single runway*! But it was a very long runway, and could handle any type of aircraft in the world: high-performance fighter-jets, commercial airliners, enormous Galaxy C-5 transports. Could have landed the Space Shuttle there, if they'd had them flying in 1971. In that year it was the busiest airport in the world. Landings and takeoffs once every ten seconds, it seemed, right around the clock. In order to reach Battalion, you had to drive down to the "approach" end of the runway. Then you had to stop and wait for the next Viet Nam Airlines 727 or Air Force C-5 or wing-to-wing pair of screaming F4 Phantoms to come in over the white line and touch down. Then the stoplight would go green and you had a few seconds to dash across the end of the runway without getting clobbered by a set of landing-gear or blown silly by slipstream.

Aircraft came in hot and high. In the last seconds of approach, they would drop out of the sky like a hurtling brick, graceless and steep, and touch down with a huge white puff of tire-smoke. Naturally, any decent pilot attempted to ground his gear right on the White Line. The precipitous final-approach was because over the years Viet Cong had hung out in the maze of slums along the upwind leg, in order to take potshots at incoming planes. Light AA rocketry, automatic weapon fire, random rifle shots. Cholon, that particular district of Saigon, was such a rabbit-warren, there was no tracking down the perps. So if you were an inbound pilot, you stayed high until the last second to make it harder on them. Whether from the hot approaches or from the Viet Cong antiaircraft, over the years there were lots of aircraft that pranged on in. So, on the way out to Battalion, one drove past an enormous heap of twisted, charred airplane fragments – fuselages and parts of wings and raggedy empennages and crumpled-up landing gear -- which had been bulldozed off the runway and piled up. I guess the subliminal idea was to horrify the more suggestible GIs, but I can just imagine the impression made on innocent civilian passengers as they winged their way to a Saigon landing past that grim, heaped-up boneyard.

And while we're on the subject of gruesomeness, there was another interesting sight on the way out to Battalion. The US Military Morgue. Combat fatalities were transported here in body-bags, cleaned up if possible, then placed in bright, plain, rectangular coffins of buffed aluminum for the somber airlift home. They were flown into Travis AFB in California, or Dover AFB on the East Coast. Draped with a flag, carried down the transport's tailramp by six uniformed pallbearers, delivered over to the disconsolate survivors. Flag folded crisply into a tight triangle, then passed over to a sad-eyed mother or wife, delivered with sober condolences. We saw it a hundred times on the Huntley-Brinkley Report...a hundred out of fifty-eight thousand. Anyway, what a jeep-driver saw on the trip out to Battalion was a huge stack of empties, twelve high, twenty wide, two hundred yards long. Empty, but poignantly somber in their implication.

Well...all that aside. Battalion HQ was a ditzy, informal mess of a compound. One expected to encounter BJ Hunnicut or Trapper John or Radar O'Reilly. There was absolutely no standing on ceremony. It was like a little trip to the beach. The motor pool would latch onto that jeep and have it spiffied-up in short order. Drivers were directed toward the clubhouse, where you could have a couple of beers at nine o'clock in the morning if you wanted to. Ignite a doobie? Sure, not a problem, if you were so-inclined. They cultivated Finest Saigon Weed right inside the perimeter. No charge. Put your feet up, relax, have lunch in the always-open mess lean-to while the jeep got serviced. The reason for the casual atmosphere, of course, was that it was so damned hard to get out to Battalion. Nobody important bothered. The little compound sat in a scrubby No-Man's-Land bounded by that gigantic runway on one side, and multiple echelons of barbed wire and land mines on the other. There were *rewards* for being isolated.

One day after a month or so at Joint Command, it occurred to me why I was always looking for chances to get out and about: I was *cold*! The building's air-conditioning kept the temperature down to a nice even eighty-one degrees. But...I'd gotten *acclimatized* to Viet Nam! Eighty-one was *darned* cold! The outside air-temp was more like a hundred or a hundred and five. With relative humidity so high, even the trees dripped condensate...even in the "dry" months between monsoons. It just felt refreshing to get out of that damned meat-locker and warm up a few times a day.

There was plenty of opportunity for me to write a nice long letter to Elle, every single day. Shortly after she started as our typist, Mai dragged a chair over to my desk. I'd been penning my daily five-pager to Elle, but I turned my stationery pad facedown and set my pen aside. Mai had brought along a notebook and her own personal Viet/English dictionary. The cover read "Viet/Anh English/Vietnamese." She sat right there next to me. She smelled like a gardenia, or maybe an orchid. She gave me a nice smile. Then she reached over and grabbed my portrait-photograph of Elle and myself in our wedding finery, taken two years before, not thirty seconds after we'd said our I-do's.

"Wife, her?" Mai asked.

"Yes. That is my wife. Her name is Elle." I delivered these sentences like it was an elementary English lesson.

Mai thumbed rapidly through her dictionary and scribbled a bit on her pad. "She very pretty, eyes...hair." she said, a trifle wistfully. Mai's eyes lingered on Elle's pouffy blonde hair and her wide, round, blue-blue eyes. My eyes took in Mai's thick, glossy raven-black hair, her flawless café-au-lait complexion, her beautiful, exotic, dark-dark eyes. I wondered why *she* should feel envy for the image of my faraway wife. But I kept my speculations to myself.

I went back to my letter. I had just finished Part A when I paused for Mai's interlude. Part A was the part where I'd commented on all the little Oregon doings and observations from Elle's last letter. Next came Part B, some obligatory observations about what was new on my end. After that, I'd wind it up with Part C which consisted of some expressions of love, of longing, of how much I missed her kisses and her warmth next to me in bed and her sexy boobs and whatnot, and what I intended to do about all that when I got back to her, in the impossibly far-away future. All my letters to Elle pretty-much hewed to that three-part outline. Well, so on to Part B, the what's-new-in-Saigon segment. I thought I ought to include some reportage about our new typist here in the Edit Shop, so I rambled on about Tuoi Mai for a short paragraph, random generalities and observations of Mai-unique quirkinesses. It lacked in detail, but did passable service to the Gods of Full Disclosure, I imagined.

"You write to wife?" Mai asked. *Where was she picking up her English?*

"Yes."

"I read?"

"Well...okay." I marked the Mai paragraph with a paperclip and handed over the letter. For fifteen minutes or so, she thrashed through her dictionary and made notes on her pad, careful not to make marks on my letter. When she was done, she handed it back to me.

She regarded me with a sober gaze. "Very kind, you," she told me, using my name in her ditzy way. She touched the back of my hand with her fingertips, just a light graze, and I flinched at the momentary flow of ectoplasmic current.

A couple weeks later – the usual turnaround-time in the letterborne conversation between Elle and myself – I got my wife's comments back on the Mai thing. "Miss Mai sounds very nice," Elle opined. That was the first, last, and only thing she said to me about Tuoi Mai, ever in her life.

13
_____

I Visit Hoi Duc Anh and Fail to Adopt a Daughter

There was another stratagem for getting outside of the icy-cold Joint Command building. That was a visit to Hoi Duc Anh.

The 252nd "Support" Company – a fairly large unit at about 400 officers and enlisted staff -- was the one single organizational subdivision of our Battalion, excepting the actual bona-fide Support personnel, referred to as "Headquarters Company". Like those motor-pool staffers, for instance. And the maintenance staff, cooks, supply organization, and administrators at the Parker Compound, until the day that little ancillary post, all inspected and approved, got abandoned, and we all upped-stakes and moved to MACV. Most of those staffers were no longer required, and were reassigned to lord-knows-what horrible duties. Ammo-carriers in a firebase somewhere in the mountains? Helicopter refuelers? Ground-pounding grunts with M16s, heaven forefend? But "Battalion" did include a necessary cadre of command-staff officers and _their_ support people...maybe another hundred, altogether. The combined group – 252nd Company and Headquarters Company -- had an ongoing Public Service Project.

Public Service was a required objective of any unit that was sufficiently permanent to be able to maintain a project of this type. You had to be involved in a non-combat mission, for the most part. You had to be nailed to one particular place. That place had to be relatively safe, which meant relatively removed from "hot" zones...and that was a tricky call in Viet Nam. The public-service project itself had to have P.R. value...like a school or a hospital or a dog-pound or something. Ours was Hoi Duc Anh, an orphanage in the middle of Saigon.

With the correct diacritical marks, the orphanage was named:

hôi đúc ánh

The words translated literally as "ask faith light", but the meaning was more like "we pray for the enlightenment of faith." It seemed an archetypally Buddhist ethos. But pan-spiritual as well. Hoi Duc Anh had been founded and staffed by a small, obscure order of Buddhist nuns. It occupied a very run-down building on a triangular property bounded by two very busy streets. A line of shabby shops along one of the streets held small business enterprises staffed by the older children, ostensibly for their vocational education...but actually for the smidgen of profit these operations contributed to the orphanage. There was a floor-tile manufactory, a beauty shop, a barber, a nail salon, a bakery. Every few days, we'd get a sackful of Hoi Duc Anh baguettes at Joint Command, fresh out of the oven, crispy-crusted and soft-sweet-tangy inside, just like one would find on a Paris boulevard, its unique recipe another of the unlikely gifts left behind by French colonialism. You could buy a fresh-baked baguette like that off a street-vendor's pushcart on your morning walk to Joint Command, two feet long and costing ten piasters...that equated to about two cents, American. But Hoi Duc Anh's French baguettes were the best. Well, at the orphanage there was a dusty play-yard with sad, overworked playground equipment – swings, sandboxes, slivery wooden climbing structure, beat-up tricycles -- set off from the other boulevard by wrought-iron fencing and shrubbery. The two-story masonry main-building housed something like four hundred and ninety orphans. Everywhere from teenagers down to newborns. Many of them bore the wounds of war, or suffered sicknesses, or wielded the stumps of amputated limbs. Many, many of them were the children of American fathers and Vietnamese mothers. The US military policy as to war-zone cohabitation was "look the other way." Official barriers to marrying a Vietnamese woman ran the gamut from overt to very, very subtle. No help or encouragement was offered in bringing your Saigon girlfriend home to the US to meet your momma. Even if your girlfriend was six months pregnant with your baby. GIs reached the end of their yearlong tour, and usually just said "Well...*Bye-bye!*" to the girl they'd spent most of that year sleeping next to and trying willfully to impregnate. If they weren't complete cads, they'd maybe leave her a fistful of dollars. Since traditional Vietnamese society was intolerant of mixed-race children, the mother's recourse was abandonment of the child to an orphanage. For all the harshnesses and injustices of the previous century of colonial occupation, the French acknowledged and took in their hybrid offspring, gave them care and schooling and recognition and access to French citizenship. Our battalion gave a little bit of material support to the twenty overworked Buddhist nuns at Hoi Duc Anh, and called it good.

Once every couple of weeks, one of the OB sergeants would sign out a 2½-ton truck with benches along the canvas-tarped back – a "deuce-and-a-half" -- and round up as many Joint Command personnel as wanted to go out to the orphanage. First though, we'd hit the Base Exchange. Buy a few bags of taffy and hard-candy and Tootsie-Rolls. Buy some toys and some T-shirts. Load up some canned food, kitchen staples, bottled water, school supplies, and basic medical needs that had been charitably put aside by the BX management. Then off to the orphanage. The kids knew the drill: all those American GIs had candy in their pockets! We'd be mobbed, shook down, stripped of the loot by a joyful, screaming throng of kiddos. Then we'd schlep the more quotidian supplies into the kitchen and the infirmary and the schoolroom. Then we'd go through the dispensary and visit the infants and the tiny floorcrawlers and the kids who were sick and the kids with no legs or no eyes and the kids wrapped up in yards and yards of bandages. *Those* kids liked candy too!

In the initial kid-onslaught as we jumped off the deuce-and-a-half that first time I went to Hoi Duc Anh, I noticed one tiny-tiny little girl 'way back in the mob. She was maybe two years old. She was maybe two feet high. Dressed in a torn-and-mended *ao dai* of faded pink rayon. Even on a tiny toddler, the traditional garb looked exotic and lovely. It may well have been the only clothing she owned. Well, she wasn't going to wind up with any Tootsie-Rolls because she'd never succeed in pushing her way through that writhing mob, even if she'd had the pluck to try. I pulled a couple out of my cargo pocket before they were all snatched away and buttoned them safely into my upper shirt pocket. When the madness abated, I went back to her and squatted down so I'd be a bit more on her level. When I produced those rolled-up chocolates, her eyes lit as if I'd had a fistful of gold and diamonds for her. She was my little limpet from then on, and on each subsequent visit to Hoi Duc Anh, she'd spot me quickly, come toddling as fast as she could in her raggedy pink *ao dai*, and glom on to my hand. All she wanted was someone to love. I spoke hardly a single word of Vietnamese yet, although Miss Mai was trying to change that, but it didn't matter because this darling little urchin spoke not a single syllable of *any* language. One of the nuns told me her name was 'Cuc,' but they did not know anything else about her. She'd been dropped off in a cardboard box outside the wrought-iron gate with a very brief note, when she was perhaps two weeks old. If I had had the means, and if I had not been only twenty-four, and pretty self-absorbed, and not particularly capable of thinking beyond my own ego and cynicism and arrogance, I would have moved Heaven and Earth to get that little mite the *Hell* out of that dreary place, and to this day I would have a lovely daughter, all grown up, named Cuc. But I didn't…I didn't. Sins of omission…they are the worst.

Miss Mai brought her notepad, pen and dictionary over to my desk one afternoon. I suspected what was up. So I put aside the novel I was reading and fetched her a chair. I fetched her a cup of OB tea, only slightly less execrable than OB coffee. On the open page of her notepad I could see sentences in English written out carefully, with counterparts in Vietnamese right below. So! She was enrolled in an English class in her off-time! She summoned her courage to the sticking-point and tried out a phrase on me. She started out with her ditzoid version of my name, which always melted me into a puddle. "Please. I try to learn English. Can you help me?"

"Of course…I'd be very pleased, Mai," I responded.

"What?" Whichever exemplar had taught her this useful utterance had evidently quacked the word rather than said it with any particular mellifluousness, and she'd copied to a T. We were going to have to work on that.

"Yes. I am happy to help you," I repeated. I'd have to

remember to keep the sentences short and simple. And speak clearly. Slow down, too. But no baby-talk or telegraphy. And none of that insulting, god-damn GI pidgin like you heard downtown in the bars.

So we started. Maybe half an hour a day. We had plenty of time in our relaxed duty-day. It eventually became clear to me that Mai would prepare herself overnight with a handful of new words, and maybe a question or two on a topic she wanted to know more about. She burned with curiosity to learn more about the United States. She wanted to know more about where I came from, this Oregon place...all she knew about the US was highly biased toward Hollywood and New York City. And she wanted to know everything about me! What was I like as a child? What was my family like? Any brothers? In the Army, like me? Any sisters? No??...so sad! Where did I grow up? ...Where go to school? What was it like, the University? How had I met my beautiful, beautiful wife? Was she ever a movie star? Or a fashion model? Her photographs in magazines? Did I have a nice car in Oregon to drive? ...A big nice house to live in? And on and on and on. What would I want to do first-thing when I went home? Never mind...I know!...too personal! What career did I want to take up, after the Army? Why did I come in the Army, anyway...and why they not make me officer? – Army *never* draft college graduates as just ordinary soldiers! [this was a widespread popular myth] Did I go on holiday a lot? Had I ever traveled to Europe, or South America? Did I like to drink beer? Whiskey? Did I smoke cigarettes? Did I do drugs, ever? Very bad in Saigon...drugs. You stay away drugs, or I write letter to that beautiful Elle wife and get you in big trouble! Did I like it here in Viet Nam? Did I like Viet Nam people? Viet Nam food? Viet Nam *girls*? Did I go to Saigon bars, ever, and mess around with Viet Nam *bar*-girls? Because, that was no good...only want money...not decent girls...bad sicknesses them, not healthy. And on and on. Her concerns were a combination of excited, insatiable curiosity tainted by massive misinformation and underlain with hopeful concern that I harbor nothing but good impressions of her country and people. And concern for my wellbeing, personally. It was so hard to give her satisfying answers in a few words, but she'd write down the key ones and ask me to make sure she'd spelled everything right. And then she'd go home that evening to look them up in her Viet/Anh dictionary. For the rest of it, we did charade pantomimes and drew stick-figure sketches and fumbled along, with mammoth misunderstandings at every turn, resolved only gradually. We both knew the silliness or our errors, and we quietly laughed and laughed together.

In riposte, I grilled her about herself. I learned that she had grown up far to the north of Saigon. A mountain town: Dalat. In her memory it was a cool green paradise. Forested, breezy. Treeclad ridges interspersed with deep, fertile valleys. Her younger days had been idyllic. She had left all that behind, and all her friends and many of her kin, when her father had moved the family to Saigon. He was a marginally successful tradesman who sold and repaired pre-owned automobiles. Dalat was gradually becoming depopulated as regional towns lost citizenry in the flight to the Capital. Country urban centers were no longer safe. Trades that had sustained many families were failing from a dearth of middle-class customers and a general shortage of disposable income as the war dragged on. Worst of all, terror and combat was becoming unpredictable...random. One never knew if one's neighbors were Viet Cong, or if the NVA were going to infiltrate en masse some dark night. Minding one's own business and staying apolitical was becoming not-an-option. After liquidating their meager assets and coming to the city, Mai's father had taken a lease on a small business premise for his car repair business at 92 Gia Long Street in Saigon's District One. The family had crowded into a tiny apartment one floor above the garage. On nights when the wind was unfavorable, fumes from the garage's diesel generator wafted into the bedroom Mai shared with her sisters, and gave her throbbing headaches.

In Saigon, it had been possible for Mai to finish her secondary schooling and then obtain some vocational training in secretarial work – reception and telephone protocol and stenography and filing and the like. And, of course, typing. She'd been sent out to find a job, for her family needed whatever additional income she could garner. Miss Mai was uncomplainingly working fifty-hour weeks for the grand sum of twenty-eight dollars a month, generously paid-out by the US Army.

All this intelligence did not flow between us in an afternoon! It took weeks and weeks, and many hilarious sessions of pseudo-communication through pantomime and many, many resorts to the translation dictionary to get the ideas across. We laughed a lot, but as privately as we could manage. We smiled and encouraged each other to say just a little more, each time we spent half an hour on what we kept pretending were English-learning sessions. The sessions gradually lengthened to an hour or more. We found ourselves looking into each other's eyes sometimes, and not knowing what it was we saw there, and not being able to resist gazing deeper. We were very careful not to touch each other at all, ever.

One day Mai took me into her confidence about a small problem: she had an *admirer*! In June, another contingent of Analysts had been assigned. Specialist Fourth-Class Travis was one of three new OB guys. He was no more than nineteen, I would guess, with wavy blond hair and rakish good looks. He was pretty certain he was irresistible. He took a shine to Miss Mai, and started wandering back to Edit from his duty desk on the far side of OB, just hanging around. He offered to help her with English lessons, evidently cued-in by the quality time she seemed to be spending with me. He started slipping her handwritten notes.

"He call me '*MY*'!" she giggled. She showed me a note from Travis, and pointed out the spelling error on her name. I felt mildly wicked peeking at another man's *billet-doux*. But indeed he'd spelled Tuoi Mai's name in the English transliteration of the syllable's sound, ignorant of the fact that in Vietnamese, 'My' would be pronounced to rhyme with "bee" or "flee". Why hadn't Travis had a look at her nametag, pinned to the front of her *ao dai* every day? Where had Travis been in March of 1968, when Lt. Calley and Charlie Company had wrought their havoc in a little hamlet named My Lai? Oh yeah...he'd been fifteen years old then, most likely. Caught up in sophomoric doings and high-school sports. Hadn't had the inclination for newspapers or Walter Cronkite reports. Else, Travis would have known how to pronounce both of the pertinent syllables properly, the right one as well as the wrong one, and then maybe Miss Mai would have looked on his amorousness more receptively. As it was, she asked me to make him leave off. Well, that was a big request, it being a dicey business man-to-man, warning a fellow soldier off of a romantic endeavor. That's probably how the Parker Compound had wound up on its interminable roast-beef diet. I did a slipshod, half-ass job of it, though, on Mai's behalf...the best I could manage. The passage of a little time handled the rest, and Travis discovered that Tu Do Street bar-girls were much more willing conquests, seemingly far more cheerfully disposed, and less virtuous by far than Miss Mai. Scanty virtue was evidently what he was looking for.

14

Franco Zeffirelli Brings Mai to Tears

W hen I lived a normal life before the US Army and my Draft Board, God bless 'em, erroneously decided I'd make a good soldier, I had amused myself playing guitar. I'd picked up the guitar young. I don't think I was more than twelve or thirteen. My older brother ragged me constantly, mocked my efforts, made ongoing, teasing commentary whenever I tried to practice in the room I necessarily shared with him. Eventually, I took myself off alone somewhere to practice and play, a victim of his acid wit.

After many years of reflection, I now know what it was that bothered my brother. I was doing something he was not capable of doing himself. He was older than me. Just...not very much older. Only fifteen months. It was not enough to give him undisputed superiority. Add to that, he and I were worlds different in personalities. It was natural I'd have interests different from his, and little successes in places he wouldn't attempt to go. Vice versa is undoubtedly true, and I admit it. But what I said before, it stuck in his craw. Hence, the mockery. Anyway, the point is, influenced negatively by the mocking, I grew into someone who was anything but a flamboyant public performer when it came to the guitar.

I preferred just strumming chords. Simple progressions. Maybe a melody line thrown in. I was never going to be particularly good at it, so I figured I'd just as well please myself. I liked to sing songs to my own accompaniment. Wasn't any outstanding star at that, either, so tended to do that in private too, for only my own entertainment. But the 'sixties and 'seventies were the Folk Revival. The University had been a hotbed of this musical movement. I had a hundred tunes in my head, all the chords and all the words. Every once in a while, there were chances to get together with others and belt out a few songs around a campfire while a big bottle of cheap red wine made the rounds. Good times, for certain. My first guitar had been a nice little compact Guild with a macramé strap I'd knotted myself, easy to play, always in-tune, and I'd taken it on many an adventure with me. I just hadn't been able to bring it with me to Viet Nam, is the only thing.

Well we had this catalog. Every GI got a copy. The Pacific Exchange catalog. PacEx for short. All kinds of stuff, mail-order. Things you couldn't get at the local Base Exchange, or that wouldn't stay in-stock for more than an afternoon assuming the BX ever got a shipment. Stereos. Tape-decks. Cameras and camera-gear. Nice jewelry and textiles to order shipped home for wives and girlfriends. Yeah, yeah…may they never meet. Most of this merchandise was Japanese or Asian in origin, but top-of-the-line. Sony electronics. Nikon and Yashica and Minolta cameras. Mikimoto pearls. Thai silk. Hong Kong tailored garments. Priced so fantastically cheap, a guy could hardly NOT buy some nice stuff out of that catalog. And on one page toward the back end, a beautiful Yamaha Classic guitar. After six weeks of guitar-withdrawal in Saigon, I broke down and ordered one.

Miss Mai was peering over my shoulder as I knifed my way into the box that eventually arrived. Our mail, instead of being dumped off at our barracks quarters in the MACV Annex, got distributed at our duty stations. When the guitar came out of the bubble-wrap, Mai gasped audibly. "You do that?" she asked in amazement. Apparently she meant, did I play one of these things.

"Uh-huh!" I assured her. In a moment it was tuned up, and I strummed-off a riff or two.

"You know, Time Us?" she asked me.

"Huh?"

"Time Us! A song, silly! No…It Us Time…or, uh--???" No use…she didn't quite have the title and her guesses weren't making sense to me. She tried to hum the theme, but gave up, laughing at herself. "You wait!" she said in delight. She hurried off to consult with Mrs. Lon in the outer OB bay. When she scurried back, she was clutching a recent copy of the Stars and Stripes, Viet Nam Edition. She thumbed wildly through the newspaper. Stopped at the page where the week's movies at MACV, Tan Son Nhut, and Annex theaters were listed. "This

113

one!" she said in triumph. She pointed at a poster advertising **Romeo & Juliet**, like all movies aired for servicemen in Viet Nam, not exactly first-run, but fairly recent. The film was opening Wednesday for a one-week run at the MACV Headquarters indoor theater.

I got a vague glimmer of what she was getting at. "Oh yeah!" I smiled. "Franco Zeffirelli! **Romeo & Juliet**! I *love* that movie!" It had come out in 1968, the summer Elle and I married, and we'd watched it that baking-hot summer, then gone back home and made frantic love like Capulets and Montagues. The name of the beautiful theme-song came to me. A Time For Us! I hummed the opening bars.

I thought Mai was going to weep! Between the two of us, we'd plucked the most sentimental nerve in that sweet girl's entire psyche. "Yes…YES! Time for Us! You do it?" she pointed at my shiny new Yamaha guitar.

I strummed a few chords. Not so hot. I plucked out the melody in the key of C…then tried G. Not much better. "Listen, Mai. Give me a couple days and I'll work the music out for you."

"What?" she asked, like a duck quacking.

A couple hours later I had a passing idea. When you went to the movies at MACV, you had to show your Army I.D. card at the box office to gain admittance. Tickets cost a whole twenty-five cents. You had to wonder why they bothered charging anything at all. Also, US civilian personnel carried I.D. that got them admittance just about anywhere Army personnel could go. If you took them as a guest, or otherwise personally vouched for them, you could get Vietnamese civilians into the theater. Lots of guys took their girlfriends to the movies.

I thrashed around on the Edit typing-desk. Found the Stars & Stripes Mai had fetched earlier. Found Mai. She was having a cup of tea with Mrs. Lon. I beckoned her into the Edit office.

"Look, Mai…would you like to go see this movie on Friday? I can get you in, if you'd like.

"What?"

Hmmm. How was I going to get this across? I wrote the

question down…she was better with complex sentences if they were written out for her. And she could always take it home and resort to her faithful Viet/Anh. I circled the picture of Olivia Hussey kissing her co-star, using my red edit-pencil, and left her to puzzle it out.

In a few minutes she approached me diffidently. "I bring girlfriend?" she asked.

"Sure! No problem!"

"Not a…a 'date'?" Her eyes strayed to the photo of Elle on my desk, as if my faraway wife might be listening in.

"Okay…not a date. I'll just get you in the theater, all right? You meet me there with your friend."

She brightened. "Okay!"

So that was how we came to be standing in line outside the MACV Cinema box office at 7:30 p.m. on a warm Friday evening in July, waiting for the theater to open up. Mai and her girlfriend, fragrant as flowers and resplendent in silken *ao dai* in line just up in front of me, pretending we weren't on a date, chattering and giggling. On up the line, maybe forty people, among them a dozen or more other young troops with a girlfriend by their side, but with a lot more handholding and arm-clinging going on up there.

An older American in Army fatigues came strolling toward the movie queue from under the Jacaranda trees just to the east. He was walking a dog on a leash. A *Doberman Pinscher*! A nice big red-and-rust male, ear-clipped and tail-cropped, well-behaved, at heel on a loose lead. I flashed on my boy Reddy and felt a momentary jab of poignant loneliness. The man wandered aimlessly, following where the dog sniffed, and wound up approaching the waiting moviegoers on up the line from me. Guys started snapping to attention and saluting. Parade-ground salutes, crisp and precise.

Uh-oh…this fellow must be pretty high-rank. I surreptitiously straightened my necktie and my cap – I'd opted for Dress Khakis and spit-shined loafers for the evening. He came ambling back my way, casually returning salutes and making small talk with three or four enlisted types as he moved along.

115

As he approached, I could see that his collar had officer's rank on it. Stars! Cripes, the guy was a *General*! Waitaminnit! *FOUR* stars! I let my eyes dart to his shirt pocket where a stitched-on green fatigue-colored sticker had the guy's name on it.

Abrams.

Christ on a Crutch! That four-star was General Creighton Abrams! Recently appointed Commander of the whole damn Military Assistance Command, Viet Nam! Decorated hero of World War II, a brilliant Division-level tank commander, second to General George S. Patton in the liberation of Bastogne! I snapped to the most rigid attention I'd ever managed in my entire, brief, unremarkable military career and ripped off my best-possible, Class-A salute.

"Evening, Specialist," the great man replied mildly, returning the salute. "At ease, please."

Then something rather interesting happened. As I snapped my hand back down to my side, the General's great, fierce Doberman Pinscher gave it a Nose Shot. DPs have a very expressive snout, and when something interests them, they give it a good bump with their big wet schnozzles – a Nose Shot. I turned my hand over, palm out, and the General's dog gave me a massive affectionate lick. Don't believe everything you hear about Doberman Pinschers!

"He seems to like you," General Abrams remarked.

"Yes Sir. I have a Dobie just like him at home." I believe I kept the shakes out of my voice.

"Do you? What's his name, Specialist?"

"Champion Marienburg's Monarch Redago, CDX. He just took a five-point major to complete his champion title. Uh...we call him Reddy. Uh...Sir. Oh...sorry, Sir...this is Miss Tuoi Mai, and her friend Miss Tuyen Thi. Ladies, this is General Creighton Abrams." The general nodded and smiled, acknowledging the introduction.

"Marienburg! There's Marienburg on this big guy's pedigree. Did you leave Reddy with your folks while you're deployed, soldier?"

"With my wife, Sir. In Oregon."

The General glanced rightward, to where Mai and her girlfriend stood wide-eyed and openmouthed. You could see the General performing some mental arithmetic. I wore Intelligence Branch brass on my collar – recently Brasso'd to a high dazzle, thank the Almighty! -- why would a therefore presumeably intelligent young man say 'my wife' out loud when standing next to a couple of pretty young Indigenous Personnel if one or the other of those Indigenous Personnel were his temporary in-country girlfriend? He seemed to come up with an acceptable sum. "Well…enjoy your movie, Specialist. Ladies? Good evening." He offered the girls a sketchy salute. The most-famous, highest-ranking military officer I ever clapped eyes on in my entire life, before or since, sauntered away, our mild conversation concluded.

"You *KNOW* him???" Mai asked in an amazed whisper.

"Uh-huh," I stammered. "General Abrams. My dad and him went to different schools together. Back home, we call him 'Uncle Creighton' whenever he stops by for drinks." Someday soon, Mai's English was going to be too good for me to get away with lying so preposterously.

We found three seats about halfway down, right in the middle. I got the girls bags of popcorn. It was stale and salty and uninspired, but they wolfed it like chocolate bonbon treats. The lights went down. Mai sat in the middle, next to me. Her warm shoulder grazed my arm and I tried to ignore the continual arcs of plasmic discharge. She graciously conceded the armrest to me.

I feel certain that a large portion of the Elizabethan English went over Mai's head. It was all right…she'd seen this film a dozen times, dubbed in Vietnamese. You could swear she was quietly aping the dialogue in that language. Her girlfriend was too. Every time the soundtrack would come up with that Time For Us theme, she'd get teary-eyed. The last time, when the tragedy of star-crossed lovers had played itself out in the Capulet sepulcher and the fatal dagger was plunged, the tears spilled over. She was beyond helping herself, and she slipped her left arm through mine, grabbed on with the right arm too, and clutched me, eyes streaming, weeping with emotion, her face buried tight against my shoulder. With my free hand I groped in my shirt pocket for a couple of spare popcorn-napkins and passed them over. Mai shared with her girlfriend Thi, who was also weeping piteously. In the dim reflected light from the screen, I took a brief visual survey, and counted at least twenty other Viet ladies crying their eyes out.

At the appropriate moment in the course of the instrumental theme song, Mai whispered the lyric in English: "Someday…a time for us…you and me." She could have been looking at me from the corners of her eyes, or I could have been imagining it.

As the house lights came back up, Mai quickly released my arm and folded her hands in her lap, all innocence. She gave me a sidelong guilty smile. Oops…sorry for losing control like that! Then she lingeringly kissed her index finger and transferred the kiss to the back of my hand. As always, I tried to deal with the phantasmoplasmic coronal discharge without flinching too badly.

I had duty every other Saturday, and the day following Mai's and my movie non-date was one such. Mai only came in on weekdays, so she wasn't there. The OB center was working on a skeleton crew. There was nothing much doing. I dinked around on guitar with A Time For Us. Made a little progress. In the afternoon I fetched my nice new Yamaha guitar home from Joint Command, and stayed up until midnight working on the piece. You'd have thought my plunking on my guitar would have kept the other guys awake until they'd have clobbered me, but the fact is, nearly all of them were somewhere else, shacked-up in cheaply-rented apartments downtown with lush, willing babes they'd met in bars. I was practically alone in that great big barracks.

On Sunday I worked on the tune some more. By the end of the day, I could make a respectable showing of the piece. Sort-of Segovia style, chords and melodic runs and a little ornamentation. It sounded pretty good. So on Monday I took the Yamaha back to the OB office. When things slacked off and the other Edit guys headed out for lunch, I lingered a moment. Mai usually brought half a papaya and some vegetables with rice for lunch, and ate it with Mrs. Lon and Mrs. Nu.

"Mai, I've got something I want you to listen to, before you go to lunch," I told her with a conspiratorial wink.

"Okay," she agreed, as if she'd understood every word. She settled herself while I reached behind the file cabinet and brought out the guitar.

I was only about halfway through the first eight measures when I realized I'd brought her to tears, just like Franco Zeffirelli had done in the darkened theater. Tears and a beatific smile…what a combination. I let her weep and she let me play. When I was done, she rummaged in her purse and dug out a hankie. Fixed herself up. Lingeringly kissed that index finger again. This time, she gently laid the finger-kiss on my mouth. "*Tôi yêu ong*," she whispered. She swept up her little plastic bag of lunch and dashed out to find Mrs. Lon.

It took me twenty minutes thrashing through the Viet/Anh dictionary to dope those syllables out. Each one, like all Vietnamese syllables, had multiple translations depending on the diacritical marks. I wasn't so sure of the spellings, even. And I obviously hadn't been able to make the marks out from just hearing her say the words. Also, the word syntax was puzzling. One of the possibilities was "*WEAK GARLIC-BULB*" but I was sure this could not be correct. But Hell! I was one of the guys who'd broken the Aggressor Code! First ever at Ft. Holabird! Captain Cameron USMC had *saluted* us! A few stinkin' little words of Vietnamese weren't going to stump the likes of me! I studied all the alternate spellings, possibilities and permutations until I found the one that made the most sense. What she'd said was:

I love you

15

I Attend the Big Hoi Duc Anh Gala

In late July the entire 252nd "Support" Company was invited to attend a gala celebration offered by the Honorary Board of Directors and its affiliated Community Support Association for the Hoi Duc Anh Orphanage. The gala was dedicated to our Battalion, which had so generously sacrificed so much, and given unstintingly of...blah, blah, so forth, so forth. Big cynic that I was, I suspected some political agenda, complicit between some of the wealthy and powerful members of the Saigon Establishment (well represented in the Orphanage's Support Organization) and the Army brass. Sounded too much like a big PR photo-op for my tastes.

Good thing the entire Company didn't decide to attend simultaneously. It's doubtful the gala's organizers were set up for 400-plus Army guests. But those of us who'd been more-or-less regulars on those deuce-and-a-halfs going out to goof with the orphans, well, we'd been rather, you might say, *encouraged* to attend. So we wore our spiffy khaki Class-A's and took a bus on over to the meeting hall.

There were nice finger-snacks prepared in the Orphanage's bakery, on croissants and brioches and slices of baguette. There was punch, tasting of mango and banana and other strange tropical fruit flavors. We shook hands and exchanged pleasantries with a lineup of Vietnamese upper-middle-class businessmen and their wives, turned out in the civilian counterpart of their Class-As, all remarkably fluent in English. I trotted out my French, even, and found a few delighted crypto-French-speakers, and we exchanged pleasantries as best we could in what we all remembered of *that* language. Then we were herded to ranks of folding chairs. There was a program of traditional Southeast-Asian dancing. Feathery gauze streamers and glitzy costumes, with swirly group movements performed by the older female alumni of Hoi Duc Anh. Then some traditional music, played on buzzy, whiny, whistley, thumpy instruments...nice and exotic, but atonal and jangly to western ears. We all smiled and applauded politely anyway. Again, the performers were older kids from the Orphanage.

Then it was time for speeches. The first two were in Vietnamese...one by the senior supervisory nun, the next by a minor government official from President Thieu's office. The Buddhist sister spoke calmly, mesmerizingly, with a beatific smile on her bland and aged features, and I wished I could have known the meaning of her words. The government official was a crisper orator, given to gesticulation...he sounded like he might have been running for office in challenging opposition to President Thieu, if ever in anyone's lifetime another ostensibly-democratic election might be held in South Viet Nam. Obviously, none of us 252nd types comprehended a word of *those* two presentations. But we smiled and applauded politely anyway. Finally, third up was one of our own, a Lieutenant Colonel I didn't recognize, but evidently an adjutant to our Battalion commander. The Colonel took the podium, fetched up a wad of notes, and started right in with his presentation.

He spoke for perhaps ten minutes. His speech was nothing more nor less than a long, detailed quantitative recitation of absolutely everything the Battalion had given to the Orphanage over the years. How many jars of petroleum jelly, how many bottles of aspirin, how many yards of bandages, how many cans of pork & beans, how many rolls of toilet paper, how many hours donated by medical personnel, how many cubic yards of concrete, how many dollars worth of toothpicks, how many Mickey-Mouse T-shirts...on and on and on. He didn't quite come out and say "You oughtta be damn stinking grateful for our generosity, goddamnit!" but the implication was strongly there. I wanted to sink through the seat of my chair, thence through the floorboards, and wind up a melted gooey puddle of shame somewhere down below the topsoil where no one could see me. I wished for Portia to clamber out of the <u>Merchant of Venice</u> libretto, forcefully wrest away the podium, and lesson our Colonel about straining the quality of mercy, which ought to have been droppeth-ing as a gentle rain from heaven rather than grudgingly handed over in the expectation of a bit more stinkin' *gratitude,* goddamnit! As I glanced around the crowded meeting-room, the expression on many's the face was the same as mine: embarrassment for the profound tastelessness of this grotesque breastbeating, this boastful running-on about how fucking *generous* the Battalion had been, and what a mammoth *sacrifice* it was, giving so much *stuff* to all these pathetic weaselly little *orphan* kids. And beyond that for me personally, as sudden and startling as one of Miss Mai's electroshock-therapy Magic Touches, reducing that embarrassment to insignificance and casting it aside, the other thing I realized came down on me as if a divine epiphany. I had been given a gift in the few, few months I'd been in this strange and trying situation called Viet Nam. A gift like a generous heartfelt donation, unsought but deserving of reverential gratitude, a blessing on both receiver and giver. The gift was that of coming to see the people of this land *as people*, not as inscrutable Asiatics or slopes or gooks or slit-eyed Commie insurgents or sex-willing bar-girls or Urban Cowboy drug-pushers or whatever other pejorative and demeaning and dismissive stereotypes they were more usually characterized as. They were people, all of them, with no appreciable differences from myself, or Elle, or my mom and dad and brothers. The full gamut. And me getting an inkling of that was a gift. There was one and only one source of that gift. And that source was the blithe and generous heart of a twenty-two-year-old typist named Miss Tuoi Mai, who even now at that exact moment was somewhere in this teeming city, wishing in her sweet heart of hearts that someday, somehow, there might be a time for us. And I, sitting there listening painfully to the closing whimpers of that asinine Colonel's speech, I started to realize just how thoroughly I had been overwhelmed, taken by storm, captured and ravished, beaten bloody and beyond mending by the ravening, butcherous Mongol Horde of Love. And me only a foolish, simple, guileless lad of four-and-twenty years. Whatever was I going to *do* about it?

I got back to the Edit office a little after three in the afternoon. Sgt. Timmons had taken a miss on the Hoi Duc Anh gala, but he was somewhere else in the building out of the Edit room when I arrived. No idea where the other two guys were off to. Miss Mai was there all by herself. She'd typed up a whole stack of awards citations, along with an especially-lengthy OpRep for the month. It was not that long before she'd round up her things and take off for the bus stop. She was just finishing up her day's work and putting the dust cover over the Selectric as I came in.

"Oh Luceee! I'm ho-ome!" I joked. She didn't get it. What she did do was try her patented knuckle-cracking thing to relieve her finger-fatigue. Instead of relief, she winced in pain.

"Hands hurt!" she explained.

I pulled my desk-chair over so we were sitting knees to knees. "Give me your hand!" I ordered her, and made gimme gestures. She hesitantly complied, and I commenced giving her my best Amateur Shiatsu Hand Massage.

I could see that Mai was enjoying it. I felt the tension draining from her overworked fingers. She sighed a bit. Then smiled. No…smirked.

"What?" I quacked.

"*Weak garlic-bulb!*" she scoffed through the smirk. Then a little more, but in Vietnamese. Evidently, back awhile, I'd left my decoding scribbles somewhere visible on my desk, and she'd had a peek.

"Yeah well…I weak-garlic-bulb you too."

"What?"

"*Tôi yêu cô*" I replied, secretly pleased that I'd used the correct gender form for the word 'you'.

Mai gently withdrew her hand. She looked at me soberly and wide-eyed a moment. Then, having considered, she gave the hand back. And I kept massaging. And we didn't say anything. After a while, she traded hands. The neglected hand was probably getting jealous. I kneaded in silence. I wiggled digits and made joints snap softly. I stroked her metacarpals, I probed her wristbone interstices with my thumbs, and I got thoroughly absorbed in the task. When in a few minutes I looked up to Mai's face, I saw that her eyes were closed, her head tipped softly back. She was breathing through her parted lips, almost gasping. The pink tip of her tongue moistened the sensuous fullness of her lips. *Was I hand-massaging my little typist toward sexual climax*? The notion was overwhelmingly erotic. But her possessing ultrasensitive, orgasmically-arousable fingers might somehow explain the phaser-stuns she seemed able to impart to me with her touch. Then, blushing, she opened her beautiful eyes and came back from the place she'd allowed herself to drift off to. She mumbled a thank-you, calling me by her wacky version of my name, and went about tidying her workspace unnecessarily.

16
I Get a Few Pix of Mai and We Go to Dinner

Another event occurred toward the end of August: I thrashed back and forth in the "cameras" section of the PacEx catalog and finally settled on the particular 35mm SLR I wanted to buy. Here's the way this worked: you'd look at all the cameras in the catalog, compare features, talk to everyone you knew who'd already bought a camera, have a good hard look at their equipment, peer through their viewfinders, fiddle with their f-stops, compare prices and pros and cons and add-on extras, and then, excruciatingly, make up your mind as to which brand you were going to buy. Fill out the order form, obtain a money order, and send it off. Committed! In the fullness of time, your camera would arrive, and all your buddies would cluster around as you opened the box. Then the recriminations would start! They all boiled down to one thing: "You moron! Why the *fuck* did you buy that particular piece of crap?"

Well I bought a Yashica with a 55mm standard lens. And a 35mm wide-angle lens. And an 80-200mm zoom lens that looked like a bazooka barrel. Flash attachment. A bunch of filters. Lens-cleaning kit. *Faux*-leather camera case. Sergeant Timmons had a look at all this stuff. "Why the *fuck* did you buy a crappy Yashica when they've got Nikons?" he opined. By way of answer, I had nothing.

Mai was pretty impressed. I let her fiddle with the settings and f-stops. Dry-click the shutter a few times. "Wait a minute!" I said. I dashed out into the OB bay and borrowed a roll of Ektachrome from a friend of mine, whose heartfelt comment was "Shoulda bought a Minolta, shithead!" I dashed back in to the Edit office and cranked that Ektachrome into my new camera. "Okay, Mai! Time to pose for the camera!"

That day she had worn a very pretty *ao dai* of dark-blue silk patterned with swirly white and magenta orchids, over the usual silky black pajama-bottoms. I posed her at the Selectric, smiling fetchingly. I had her stand against the wall. I got a nice head shot.

Radiant, adorable smiles, all three times. "Thanks, Mai!" I told her. "I have better photograph. At home. I give you…tomorrow."

On the following day, when no one else was around but me, Mai rummaged in her small cluttered purse. She fetched up a plain brown envelope about four inches square. Shook out a wallet-size photo. It was black-and-white. A professional studio portrait. In the photo, Mai had been a few years younger, maybe eighteen or nineteen. It was probably the Vietnamese analog to the traditional US high-school "Senior Picture." The photographer had focused-in on Mai from the neck up. Her hair had been longer in those days, a lush sweep of black-black silk. The photographer, obviously a master of his art, had opted for a dark background, and half of Mai's face was shadowed. He had her tip her face down a bit, but look upward and to her left. Her expression is serious and perhaps a little sad. There is a glinting highlight in each iris. The girl in the photograph is so breathtakingly lovely that, had I never met Mai in life, I would have fallen in love by virtue of this image alone. I have kept that photograph in my wallet for forty years. Were a mugger to rob me of my wallet at knifepoint in a dark alley some night, Mai's photograph is the only thing of value I'd regret losing.

In time, I burned up the rest of that Ektachrome and sent it in for processing. I piteously regret not having burned it up, all thirty-six frames, on images of Mai. All I came away with was three exposures of her. They were developed as 35mm slides, and just who has equipment for projecting *slides* anymore? Recently I've had them scanned into digital images…cost me six bucks. Isn't technology grand? These pix show Mai smiling, demure, youthful, energetic, curvy, sensual…ah, I could rattle off adjectives all afternoon. Lord, how I treasure those images.

When I got the film back from the lab, I naturally let Mai flip through the pix. You had to hold those little cardboard-framed slides up to the light and squint. She thought she looked ordinary and homely, and she begged me to pitch those three slides into the trash. I scoffed, slipped the pix out of her sight. A subject-change was in order. I yanked open a desk drawer and pulled out some black-and-whites of me that I'd been accumulating, prints I'd made in my off-time on the enlarger at the MACV craft-shop's photo lab. Mai leafed through this pile of images with enthusiasm. "I have?" she asked.

"Sure...any you like."

She set aside one photo of me standing next to a map and pointing, as if I was briefing my good buddy Creighton on the current military situation in Southeast Asia. Another one, snapped over a seatback of me sitting on a bus bench, looking painfully sober and about fifteen years old, concentrating on a little scrap of paper in my hands. It looks for all the world as if I'm rolling a joint...but I <u>swear</u> it was a letter from Elle that had my attention so absorbed. A third, a small 2x3 wallet pic of me, taken, like hers, by a professional photographer a few weeks before my graduation from high school, and me certifiably only seventeen years of age. Looking about twelve, however. And my oh-so-sober Basic Training graduation pic, all resplendent in Class-A greenie uniform and big formal peaked-hat decorated with an eagle or something. Maybe one or two others, all of them with me in US Army fatigues. Like my little trove of Mai-pix, those are the only ones she had of me. I hope she kept them safe, near her heart.

I would have loved for her to have had a snapshot of the two of us together. Laughing over one sundae and two spoons in a café somewhere. Or walking arm-in-arm across a Saigon bridge, widemouthed with surprise upon suddenly being ambushed by some friend with a box-Brownie. Or off on a date, in formal dress, corsage on her breast, smiling at each other. Any of those thousands of ingenuous poses that people take when they are next to someone with whom they are hopelessly in love.

"Mai..." I blurted. "Mai...would you let me take you out to dinner one evening?"

She carefully set down the photograph she'd been examining. "Out? A restaurant in Saigon?"

"That's what I had in mind. Yes."

"Bring a friend, me?" Her syntax deserted her under duress.

127

"No. Just you and me."

"But...not a date?"

"No...you would probably have to call it a date."

"What?"

"Yes a date."

She had been moving from the lighthearted to the unquestionably sober as this exchange proceeded. She pondered a moment. Then, after uttering my preposterous name, she essayed an answer: "Let me think. I tell you tomorrow."

When tomorrow eventually arrived, I waited for her to give me her answer. She let me stew and fret for most of the day. Then she made a diffident, diagonal approach to where I sat at my desk, listening to Joni Mitchell on headphones. She gently lifted the phones from my ears. "Dinner only? No dance in night clubs?"

"Dinner only."

"No liquor drinks?"

"Promise."

"You meet me downtown?"

"Wherever you'd like."

"No one see us?"

"No one see us."

There they were: the Conditions of Acquiescence, laid out on the table. "Okay," she said at last. "We have dinner, you-me!"

So a couple days later, on a warm Saigon Saturday night, I showered and shaved and made myself highly presentable, then took a little blue-and-yellow taxicab to the glitteringly-lit *porte-cochere* of a renowned Saigon hotel, where Mai had agreed to meet me. I assured the doorman that I was only there to meet a friend and that he need not take any notice on my account. I stood about, loose-limbed. I was five or ten minutes early. Nervous as a cat.

Oh lord! This was baaaad! Not twenty feet away, lounging against the building side, stood Specialist Marsden! I sidled over. "Hey, Ernie! So...what's up?" I asked him.

"Waiting to meet some friends. We're heading down to

Cholon for dinner. Gonna meet some girls from the Good Bar." This was a little dive on Tu Do Street, much-favored by OB personnel. Cheap beer: Ba Muoi Ba – Beer Thirty-Three -- the local brand. '*Good* Bar' alright...*good* place to catch the clap. "What's up with you...want to come along?" Specialist Marsden asked.

I begged off. Decided not to reveal that I was here to connect with Miss Mai, who of course knew Specialist Marsden quite well, and vice versa. My hope was that Marsden's party would come along soon, and that Mai would <u>not</u>.

Ten minutes passed. Then ten more. Marsden's gang showed up, five of them crammed into one teeny blue-and-yellow taxi. Upon spotting me, there was a lot of very loud, rude japery. Marsden crammed into the cab too, and it rolled off. Mai was late.

Ten more minutes passed, and another ten. Mai was *really* late. It was reaching the time where I thought maybe I had been stood up. Something had arisen, or she'd reconsidered the forwardness of our going out to dinner, or her strong proclivity toward shyness and propriety had overwhelmed her and she'd decided she just couldn't rendezvous with a married American serviceman, no matter her feelings on the issue. I decided to give it another ten minutes, then slink on back to the barracks.

A diminutive blue-and-yellow taxicab slid to a stop out at the curb. The backseat side window lowered three inches. A hand beckoned. And a face appeared behind the windowglass. Mai! I quickly walked over, and she pushed the door open for me.

I'd barely gotten the door closed again when she whispered, "Marsden! What *he* do here?" There was a note of terror in her voice.

"Just incredible bad luck, Mai. He was waiting for friends. He didn't see you, don't worry. Have you been just riding around in this taxi for half an hour?" I wasn't sure how much of that she got. It didn't seem to calm her very much.

"I go home now. Must go home." She was pretty freaked-out.

"Mai...there's nothing to worry about. Look...I have reservations for us at *La Cave*." This was rumored to be the nicest GI-friendly restaurant in the downtown area. "Would you be okay if we just went there? Some dinner? No Marsden, I promise!"

Well, it must have calmed her down a little. She rattled something officious to the taxi-driver, who popped the clutch and took off toward *La Cave*. I noted that Mai was wearing American-style evening clothes: a crisp, ruffled white blouse over a black mini-skirt, taupe stockings with a subtle pattern, calf-length black patent boots. She looked divine. Smelled even better.

When the cab pulled up to the curbside at *La Cave*, I shoved a handful of piasters at the driver, overpaying egregiously. You could tell by Mai's expression that she was appalled at this largesse and was taking a mental action-item to bring me into hand. American GIs, even us mere Speedy-Fours, were paid so lavishly that we were walking, talking millionaires by Saigon standards. My $280 a month would have placed me in the top two percentile of income, had I been a citizen of Saigon. It was one of the things that made us so intrinsically arrogant before the eyes of our Vietnamese allies, as well as in our own smug eyes. And so irresistible in the eyes of all those Saigon bar-girls. But undeserved obscene wealth aside, it made no sense to spoil the help.

I handed her out of the cab. She was so pretty in her Western-style attire…I'd never seen her in anything but *ao dai*. She gave me a little 'go-on-ahead' gesture. Then she fell in, a pace or two behind me.

There was a beefy doorman, or perhaps bouncer. He pulled the door back for me. Said something in rapidfire Vietnamese to Mai. She reddened, stepped inside hurriedly. "What did he say to you?" I asked her.

"Nothing…" she said in a small voice. "Nothing. Never mind." Her face said otherwise.

We went up a short flight of carpeted stairs. Met by the maitre'd. I gave him my name, told him we wanted booth seating for two. He pretty much just stood there.

Mai rummaged in her purse. "You have to give him some money," she explained in a whisper. I had a 500-piaster note in a shirt pocket, so I put my hand over Mai's before she could dig out some of her own cash. I handed over a tip. Or was it, bribe? I had

130

a bit of experience tipping headwaiters in classy restaurants before, but I'd always understood the practice was to see how excellent the attention turned out to be, and then proffer the tip *after*. A *before* tip only made sense if tables were in short supply and you didn't have a reservation.

The restaurant *La Cave* was crowded, noisy and smoky. To one side, a combo whanged out Beatles tunes in imitation of Western rock-bands. Their chief virtue, if it could be called that, was volume. Mai and I were *not* going to have any intimate conversations over our supper with such a racket.

When our waiter came by, Mai held a high-speed conversation, not bothering to peek at the menu. She delivered up a decision, apparently her order. The waiter turned his gaze to me.

The menu was wordy, pretentious. Entrees were listed in Vietnamese and in French. How, I wondered, had this joint gained a following among US Army personnel? Well, here again my nodding acquaintance with French came to the rescue. I scanned until my eyes stopped at *crevettes*. Shrimp! That would do fine. *"J'ai besoin des crevettes sautés en beurre garlique, s'il vous plait. Aussi peut-être, une petite salade niçoise."*

"Bon, m'sieu" the waiter replied.

Well maybe this wasn't going too badly after all, I thought. Foolish me.

Mai had ordered a cream soup. With slivers of fish, I believe. It arrived along with my salad. As the waiter placed her shallow, brimming soup bowl on the porcelain charger in front of her, a gout of soup slopped over the edge and down the front of her lovely, frilly blouse.

She gaped in shocked surprise. Mopped at herself with the napkin from her lap. Looked into my eyes with an expression of desperate ignominy, as if she herself had been to blame for that trivial accident. Any moderately well-trained waitstaff would have apologized profusely and produced a damp cloth for madame's blouse and would not have stopped apologizing for five or ten minutes. Our waiter, the cretin, said something to Mai in quicktime Vietnamese that made her blush scarlet. She leapt from her chair in distress and headed off toward the Ladies' Powder-

Room in something just short of a run.

"*Le Maitre'd, s'il vous plait. Ici. Plus vite!*" I told the waiter. He scurried off. In a moment, that snooty functionary came over. "Mademoiselle has had drops of soup dripped on her blouse. Be so kind as to have your receptionist go into the Ladies' Room and attend her."

"Yes sir. Right away sir."

"And Mademoiselle's dish of soup will have become cool when she returns. See to serving her a fresh dish, won't you? Suitably hot."

"Yes sir. Of course, sir."

But there was no salvaging the Worst Date Ever. I cannot imagine what gratuitous insult was offered-up to my sweet companion – twice! – by *La Cave*'s help. But I suspect it dwelt on the presumptive morals of a young, pretty Vietnamese girl of obvious decent upbringing out for a Saturday-night assignation with an American serviceman.

Mai had pulled herself together with a certain grace when she returned to our table, and we both pretended to ignore the damp blot on the front of her blouse. We worked our way through *crevettes* and *soupe de poisson au crème,* declined dessert and aperitifs and espresso. I handled the check and the tipping with as much aplomb as I could manage while Mai practically fled for the exit.

At the bottom of the entry stairs, before pushing out through the swinging doors and again encountering that doorman or bouncer or whatever he was, I stopped Mai by her sleeve. She turned to me and gave me a very tentative hug. I smelled the fragrance of her midnight-black hair...the top of her head coincided with my nose-level very conveniently. "I'm sorry, Mai," I murmured. "Everything turned out badly."

She turned her lovely eyes up to me. "No...no. I like...really!" It did not seem as if her face matched her words. She essayed my name with her usual weird, warped lack of precision. "You stay here? Please? Let me get taxi, me alone." Without waiting further, she pushed out into the warm night. I gave her the space of maybe thirty long breaths, all the while mentally kicking myself in the ass for the worst-botched dinner-date of my life. When I went out to the sidewalk, she was gone.

17

Mai Has a Few Words for Me

I got in to Joint Command early on Monday. Sat and meditated, waiting for Mai to arrive. Eight o'clock and no Mai. Five after eight, and here came a handful of other civilian employees, all of them busriders. But where was she? Eight-thirty and no Mai. At quarter to nine, I wandered out into the OB bay, wandered over to Mrs. Lon's desk.

"Mrs. Lon...Mai hasn't shown up yet. Do you—"

"Sick today," she said curtly. Inexplicably, she fixed me with a rather stern glare, so I retreated. Wandered back to the Edit office. Spent the day moping through my clerical duties, and doing a perfunctory job of typing a few award citations that Mai would have rattled off at 80 wpm. Listened to some CSN&Y on the headphones. Stephen Stills advised me that if I couldn't be with the one I love, love the one I'm with. I glanced into the blue, blue eyes behind the glass of Elle's framed photograph and felt twice as much like a pile of shit as I had before. Thanks a lot, Stephen! At five of six, I covered the Selectric and slunk on out of there. The six p.m. shuttle had left a bit early, so it was either walk two miles or flag down a lambro. I risked the perils of Saigon street-warfare and walked it.

After a supper at the Thousand-Man Mess, which I did not taste at all, I wandered around the MACV Annex. I have not yet described the place I lived for the better part of a year. The Annex was maybe a hundred acres inside a chain-link perimeter with barbed-wire on top. To the south, a short hundred-yard walk through the bougainvillea trees, the big sprawling MACV Compound. I've spoken of the Compound's indoor movie theater, and of course one can surmise that there was a nice bungalow tucked away under the Jacarandas to serve as Saigon quarters for General Creighton Abrams. And his dog. Halfway down the bougainvillea path, there was a large opening with a big square concrete helipad. This helipad was perhaps one hundred feet as the crow flies from where I lay down my head and slumbered every night for a year. Do you remember the newsreel footage from April of 1975, where hundreds of desperate Vietnamese civilians are scrambling to the top of the US Embassy Building in downtown Saigon, desperate to bail out on one of those Huey helicopter-gunships before the North Vietnamese Army stormed into town and stood them up against the nearest wall and machine-gunned them? And the similar footage of the *very last* helicopter, taking off from a concrete helipad set amongst a grove of flower-covered bougainvillea trees, with writhing, desperate Vietnamese civilians clinging to the skids? Do the arithmetic. One hundred feet from where I slept and dreamt, the last, last throe of a two-decade nightmare.

To the north, a lush-green, tree-covered private golf course. *Le Golf Club de Saigon* – a lovely linguistic mixup, that name! It sported a clubhouse and restaurant which was quite good. Always welcoming to us GIs, they poured a generous gin-and-tonic and served very good Chinese dinners alfresco on a broad veranda overlooking the first tee. Me and a few of my buddies would stroll on up there for dinner once or twice a month, and tip the headwaiter and table staff lavishly so they would remember us and continue their standout service. Well, back to the Annex. There were perhaps eighty two-story barracks, just like the crappy ones at Long Binh in which I'd spent my first wretched six days in-country, but a lot better maintained. Each barracks accommodated sixty enlisted personnel. In all, the MACV Annex could house five thousand, but by late 1971 with troop levels significantly drawn down, there were perhaps only fifteen hundred men still in residence. "In residence" is not too accurate, for as I've already mentioned, many of the guys took Vietnamese women as live-in girlfriends and moved into town. Not strictly allowed, on paper, but no one ever said a word about it.

The Annex offered an array of entertainment options. There was a fitness center with a nice, Olympic-sized swimming pool. A nice craft-shop with leatherworking tools, balsa models, lapidary equipment, art supplies, lost-wax silvercasting setup, and a well-equipped photo lab available to all comers, so long as they were carrying a military ID card. A Service Club pouring ten-cent beers and fifteen-cent mixed drinks – the Army's philosophy was "better an alcoholic than a doper." An amphitheater and performance stage, whereon five nights a week a band would attempt to imitate the Rolling Stones while a bevy of pseudo-strippers would take it off down to, but not including, their undies. These 'entertainers' were invariably from the Philippines or from Hong Kong, and were hired by the USO to tour around the Pacific in an endless loop, conceivably until they grew exhausted and old. If all these attempts at GI entertainment sound a bit dreary, I assure you – *they were*! But the effort was to keep the GIs out of the bars, the strip-joints and whorehouses, the steambath/massage/blowjob parlors, and the *really* lowclass enterprises that lined both sides of Tu Do Street, not a mile outside the gate.

Oh, and then there was the Annex Outdoor Movie Theater. On that lonely Monday night, my aimless steps took me past the theater just as the evening's feature was starting, a film that had made the rounds of many Army movie-facilities and had just come boomeranging back around to the Annex.

Franco Zeffirelli's **Romeo & Juliet**.

What the hell…I had twenty-five cents to spare.

The Outdoor Theater had seats, of course, and since it rained frequently and torrentially, there was a sort of shelter made of treated timbers and corrugated-steel roofing high-up over the seats. The screen was out there thirty or forty feet, out in the weather. The projector was in back of the tiers of seats, in a booth whose front side was one large sheet of Plexiglas. The only design flaw was that the projector's beam shone through the Plexiglas toward the screen, and in its passage it illuminated a large square *on* the Plexiglas. This was Viet Nam! In the *tropics*! A brightly-lit rectangle of Plexiglas, basically in the outdoors, was going to attract a *lot* of bugs. And live, squirmy, flitty bugs were going to attract a lot of…

GECKOS!

So, one additional entertainment aspect of watching movies in the Annex Outdoor Movie Theater was the parade of gecko-images projected to a dinosaurian twenty feet in length on the screen. It was traditional to hoot and cheer for each new gecko that rambled

136

onto John Wayne's face, and boo when a thirty-foot Projectionist's-hand would appear, rapping on the inside of the Plexiglas and shooing it away. That particular evening, the geckos seemed to have an affinity for Olivia Hussey. 'Juliet's' face was blotched by many's the gecko. Something in the surreal absurdity of all this got me to laughing at my own case of the megrims, and by eleven o'clock even the ultimate death-dealing dagger seemed somehow a little funny. I got myself off to bed in somewhat improved spirits. Let tomorrow wait upon itself.

Back at the Edit office, Tuesday was a repeat of Monday. By 8:30 still no Mai. I figured she was sick again today. I wondered if Mrs. Lon could get a note to her if I dashed over to the BX and got a nice card or something. But at quarter to nine, in she glided.

"Sorry for late," she mumbled to Sergeant Timmons. "Good Morning, Specialist Marsden," she said to my colleague. She stared at him squinty-eyed for a moment, looking for a reaction. If Ernie had so much as twitched an eyebrow, I have no doubt Miss Mai would have run weeping from the room, probably never to return. "Good morning," she said to me in barely a whisper.

"Good morning, Miss Mai. Glad you are feeling better today."

We didn't speak again until noon. As each of my three colleagues went off to lunch, one at a time, Mai carefully watched their departures. Then we were alone. I knew she had something to say to me.

"Mai, I—"

She stopped me and melted me into my usual compliant puddle with the sound of my own name, spoken in her unique fashion. "I say something. Take all day yesterday, decide what I say. Go through Viet/Anh like...like...." She imitated flipping pages like riffling a deck of cards. I could see tears starting in her dark, exquisite eyes. I found a half-packet of Kleenex in my cluttered desk drawer and offered her one. "Mai...please don't cry," I begged her.

"I am not cry! Will not! I cry already, all day at home yesterday. Sunday too, before. All night in my bed, three nights.

137

You listen me! I want be your lover. I *love* be your lover, *forever*! But…we cannot be lovers – we *cannot*! We try, we make soon everything sad. And love fly away. *Tôi yêu ong,* oh yes…but we can never be lovers. We cannot!"

"I know, Mai," I whispered. I was almost unable to talk. "I know." I do not think I have ever felt lower in my life.

Then she asked me the one thing in the world that would have made me feel a little better. "Will you let me be your sister?"

The Vietnamese for "sister" is *chi*. When one addresses an unmarried woman, one would properly say *cô Mãi*. Were she married, it would be *ban Mãi*. You call your sister *chi Mãi*. She explained all this to me, did Miss Mai. She told me that from that moment on, it would please her immensely if I'd call her *chi Mãi* when no one else was listening: my sister Mai. I do not know if this may have been a secret subterfuge common to young Vietnamese women in order to deal clemently with rejected suitors, but I have never cared. We had made a pledge to each other, a bond. Something so, so less than we desired, but something far more than only friends. She: my sister. I: her brother.

18

My R&R with Elle

Toward the end of October, I would have been in-country seven months. A Viet Nam tour was typically one full year. After six months, you were up for a seven-day R&R. By 1971, the half-dozen R&R destinations from earlier years had been pared-down to three: Bangkok, Thailand, or Sydney, Australia, or Honolulu, Hawaii. The Army would put you on a flight to one of these destinations, and fly whatever was left of you back to 'Nam after seven days. No charge, either way...but other than that you were on your own costwise. In Hawaii, you could room & board at Fort DeRussy for free – no deal like that was available at either of the other two destinations. I leaned heavily towards Hawaii, since it was not impossible to have Elle fly on out and join me. Fort DeRussy was – and *still is* – about forty acres of prime real estate right smack on Waikiki Beach, jealously clung-to by the military as a recreation center. Any particular year the US Government decides to surplus Fort DeRussy and auction this prime parcel off, us overburdened citizens will not have to pay a cent in taxes. Maybe for two or three years, in fact. What was once marshland when the Army took it over as a coastal defensive battery a hundred years ago is now worth a billion dollars a square foot. Well, in 1971 the brochures for Fort DeRussy looked a little like the Long Binh Replacement Center, only with coco-palm trees, so I was not too impressed. For a while, I turned my attention to Sydney.

The buzz about Sydney was that it was horribly expensive. Getting out to the Australian countryside was a possibility, of course, but having come from the Pacific Northwest, I wasn't too impressed with Aussie countryside terrain. Looked pretty arid in the pix. New Zealand would have been another story. However, either one of these would have run up an exorbitant airfare for Elle...more money that either one of us, or both of us together, were liable to scrape up. Not Australia then. What about Bangkok?

The deal with Thailand was that wives were discouraged. Wives were discouraged, because Thailand was pretty much Sex Disneyland for any military personnel with a loose zipper. Not that I had that loose a zipper, but still! Story was, when you got off the plane in Bangkok and made your way through the airport, you ran a gauntlet of beautiful, sexy Thai Rent-a-Girls. Crook your finger toward your choice, haggle a bit over fees, and you had yourself an, ahem, 'escort' for the week. At the end of your R&R, she'd drive you back to the airport, kiss you farewell lingeringly, accept her fee plus any tip you might think she deserved, then back to The 'Nam with you. A couple weeks of penicillin injections, and what you'd still have were lovely memories of a Bangkok idyll. Well, attractive as that option may have sounded, it would be a hard sell to Elle over the opportunity for a week in Hawaii. I put in my papers for Honolulu.

Toward the end of September, the Army initiated a new policy, called Seven&Seven. Back in Mainland duty stations, a person accrued leave at the rate of so many days a month. You could put in for a three-day pass, or a week, or whatever your CO would approve. In Viet Nam this was not available. Oh, you accrued the leave all right...you just *couldn't take* any of it. Other than maybe a two-day in-country R&R to Vung Tau or Cam Ranh Bay, oceanfront resorts, sort-of, on the South China Sea. Well, Seven&Seven changed that policy a little, and let you take seven days of leave if you'd accrued that much, back-to-back with your freebie seven-day R&R. The big deal about this was, it was a sufficiently-long leave that they'd fly you back stateside for a fourteen-day stay! Anywhere on the Mainland you wanted to go!

Hmmm. Let's think about this. Two weeks back in Oregon with Elle, versus one week in Hawaii. Mainland: no need for an airticket for Elle, no pricey Hawaiian beachfront hotel room-rentals, no costly luaus or sunrise pineapple breakfasts, no high-priced fizzy rum drinks, versus Hawaii: all that expensive stuff. Put in those terms, there was only one reasonable choice.

Screw the Mainland...let's go to Hawaii!

The clinchers were (a) a week later, the Army promulgated a revised order and said, "Aw shucks, fellers...you can take your

140

Seven&Seven at any of the three non-Mainland R&R destinations if you want to"; and (b) I'd considered what a bummer it would be, spending two weeks at home in Oregon, and then climbing back onto an airplane carrying me back to Ol' Viet Nam. Yeah…Hawaii was the one.

How did Mai figure into all this? To begin with, I didn't think I ought to keep my upcoming leave a secret from her. I've always had a hard time with calculated duplicity. She'd figure something was up anyway when I disappeared for two weeks. She showed admirable sisterly enthusiasm when I told her about the options, and about my choices so far, and about Elle's excitement regarding our rendezvous. Why would she not? All she had ever demonstrated was virtuous propriety, in spite of the affection that had sprung up between us, and all she wanted was for me to live contented and morally upright myself…and to be happy. My faraway wife Elle was an integral part of this for me. Why would Mai not try to show enthusiasm?

When I brought in a pile of tour and hotel brochures from the R&R Planning Office, she pitched in and offered her opinions. The flyers for the over-the-top glitzy resorts she tossed in the wastebasket. It became obvious she was on the hunt for Romantic Getaways. Elle, at least, was going to get the best out of me…*some* lucky girl had to! She decided I should spend a couple days in Honolulu, in a comfortable but not-too-expensive hotel, on the hypothesis that Elle and I would be unlikely to get out of bed very much for those first days. Then we should sky-up and head for Kauai. Coco Palms Resort. Queen Ka'ahumanu accommodations, overlooking the lily pond. Well, when Mai had her mind made up, there was no point in further discussion. It was a darn fine plan anyway. I booked the arrangements.

On October 12, a year to the day since I'd reported for induction, I stepped off an airplane into the lush, perfumed air of Honolulu. And into the waiting perfumed arms of my wife. There's no point in recounting the delights of the next fourteen days, because anyone who has ever been months apart from a loved one knows how everything seems magical, adventures seem to pop up serendipitously, and time rushes away with frightening rapidity. If only the eight agonizing weeks of Basic Training could have flown so swiftly. Neither Elle nor I had been to Hawaii before. It was paradise. It was relearning each other, rediscovering some mislaid magic. All too soon, we were back in Honolulu after our blissful time at Coco Palms, one more night in the Waikiki Travelodge before both of us had to get on our respective jet aircraft and fly in separate directions.

In the small hours of that last Hawaiian night, the fragrances of the tropics borne through the open windows on the night breeze, I dreamed of Mai.

She wasn't at Tan Son Nhut Airport to sweep me into her embrace. I hadn't expected her to be. But when I stumbled into the OB shop the following day, half an hour late, all jet-lagged and disoriented, she *did* leap up from her typing desk, scattering papers all over. It looked as if she was going to throw arms around me, and damn the consequences, but she aborted the action at the last second. All in attendance were treated to three or four delighted repetitions of Miss Mai's goofy rendition of my name. "I'm so happy, you come back safe!" she purred. There were numerous eye-rolls from the audience.

I'd brought her a little gift. A slim gold ring, sand-cast and brightly burnished. Dolphins circling her finger. It fit like it had been made for her. She looked as if she might weep, but she kept it together. As long as I continued to know Mai, she would bring that ring to work in an empty pill-bottle in the bottom of her purse, and slip it onto her finger, first thing in the morning. Ring finger, left hand…where loving sisters are supposed to wear golden bands, I guess.

What was the deal with the pill bottle, I wondered? Mai had never yet asked me escort her home, nor to drop by for a visit, nor yet had I met her mother or father or any of her sisters. Perhaps there was a compelling reason they should not know of our affection for each other. Perhaps they weren't even privy to my existence. Whether yes or no, I would never discover. It was a subject I did not want to quiz her about.

As the midpoint of November came and went, an ominous realization set in for Mai. I was not immune to it...the impending occurrence would affect me as well. Mai had received an eight-month appointment to her typist position. Back in the early spring, she'd made application to a civilian organization under contract to provide certain classes of labor to the US forces. She'd had to undergo interviews with that organization...and pass over a small gratuity for further consideration. Okay...it was a bribe. Standard procedure. Then she'd had to be vetted through some routine security screenings. And then, considering the secure nature of the mission of Joint Command, some not-so-routine screenings. Last, an interview with Army personnel specialists, with the intercession of a translator. But seven of those months had now elapsed. Her appointment was due to expire shortly.

Colonel Childers called Miss Mai into his office and had a private chat with her about the possibility of staying on a few more months. He was not very encouraging. All over Viet Nam, US Forces were ratcheting back. It was called Vietnamization: turn the war over to the South Vietnamese. Get the troops home now, in airplanes. Wasn't that what Abbie Hoffman had suggested as an exit strategy in about 1968, shortly after the bloody debacle of the Tet Offensive? Maybe somebody else. Not important. So, the need for indigenous personnel as temporary typists was on the wane as well. Nevertheless, the good Colonel said he'd put together a letter to the placement agency extolling Mai's abilities, particularly the amazing improvement in her English, and maybe they'd make an exception in her case.

The Colonel's letter turned up in the Edit in-box the following morning, for immediate typing. Letter-perfect, naturally. Mai contemplated the thing for ten minutes without moving a muscle. Then she glided over to me. "I cannot. Letter is about me. I cannot type." Again, she ditzed-up my name. "...You do for me?"

So I scooched my chair up to the Selectric. Clicked on the power. Rolled in a sheet. Started typing. Naturally, I botched a word in the fifth line. It wasn't in me to cuss and rage, and I didn't even wad the hashed-up letter. I just rolled it on out, scaled it gently into the Classified Waste bag, and rolled in another sheet. Four tries and I got it right. Well...sort-of right. I found myself overwhelmed by strong feelings on the matter discussed therein, and inserted two – no, *three*! -- somewhat more forceful modifiers in strategic locations.

Colonel Childers signed the letter

A week later, Master-Sergeant Thompson wandered into Edit. "Specialist," he said to me, "can you tell Miss Mai that we got a phone call from—"

"Excuse me, Sergeant," I interrupted. "You should be able to tell her yourself. Her English is pretty good these days. And anyway, it's not like I speak Viet or anything." How had I taken on the cachet of Special Translator to Miss Mai? Maybe it was that French and Russian incident, 'way back in April, creeping into the prevailing mythology.

"Hmm. Okay then. Miss Mai, your hiring agency has asked that you come downtown and have a talk with them about extending your typist contract."

She'd gotten the gist, at least. "When I come?" she asked the Sergeant.

"This afternoon. Two o'clock. Specialist, can you drive her? Take the No. 16 jeep...they just cleaned it up, out at Battalion."

Not any spur-of-the-moment work-detail assignment ever yet dumped on me by any NCO could have given me greater pleasure.

The weather in Saigon that afternoon was absolutely blissful. Mai and I strolled out the front doors of the Joint Center. "Wait here in the shade," I suggested. She lingered under the corrugated-metal awning while I went to fetch the jeep.

The upholstery of an Army jeep is utilitarian, to say the least. No. 16 had been cleaned up, with all the road dust vacuumed out and the paint job, such as it was, washed down. Not exactly hot-wax detailing, but not too bad. That front seat, however... 'shotgun' position? The canvas was pretty disreputable. I'd brought along my field jacket in case it was chilly, but it was apparent I wasn't going to need it. I'd had visions of gallantly offering my topcoat to Mademoiselle if she showed the slightest chill, as if it were an Alpaca tuxedo. Instead, I spread it over the grungy seat, and tucked it in a bit. Walter Raleigh, helping Queen Liz across a mudpuddle on his cloak.

When I got back around to the front of the building, Mai had fetched a silky white scarf out of her purse and had done up her hair for the ride. It was hard to believe anything could have made that girl look more eye-catching than usual, but the scarf did it. I jumped out and handed her in. This was not necessarily chivalric gallantry…an Army jeep is a bit of a step, even in fatigues. It was wonderful to have her hand in mine.

Fired up the jeep. Eased out the clutch. Zoomed out the gate with a backhand wave to the guards…they didn't much care about *departing* vehicles. Made a right on Nguyen Van Troi, with considerable alacrity in view of the rapid approach of a very large, mud-covered tanker truck. Around the Third Field Hospital Helipad triangle. Up the cross-boulevard toward downtown. The Master-Sergeant had given me a little sketch-map to Mai's hiring-agency, and I'd committed it to memory.

The day was absolutely fine. Sunny, with mere wisps of cloud, a pleasant temperature, no rain anywhere on the horizon. Traffic was moderate. The rottener stenches of the city had taken the day off, and all we smelled was fresh, damp soil, the pungence of charcoal smoke, crisp odors of broiling meat, and a riot of floral aromas. Trees shed blossoms like orange and yellow snow. I imagined that myriad eyes tracked our passage, took note of the lovely lady who sat on my right side, smiling and gazing around as if she'd never seen this city before. And tracked me, who must surely be the most fortunate US GI in all of Saigon, to escort such a princess. Too soon, we reached the office building. I had been warned not to leave the jeep unattended. I parked along the curbside, not thirty feet from the address Mai needed. "I have to stay here, Mai. You just take whatever time you need…no hurry, okay?"

"Okay," she assured me. Then she hopped lightly on out and disappeared inside.

Time passed. Traffic rumbled by. Pedestrians came in floods, then in trickles, then floods again. A tsunami of schoolkids all in uniform: blue shorts and white shirts for the boys, blue pleated skirts, white blouses, blue knit sweaters for the girls. Great masses of them, chattering and laughing. A fellow came along in a raggedy set of fatigues. Hopped up into my jeep! Right into the seat that Mai had vacated! I was about to react with forcefulness when I saw that both his hands were gone entirely, nothing but ruddy, rounded wrist-stumps left. The fellow smiled broadly, revealing bad teeth. He fumbled a sign tied around his neck on a piece of string, his predicament making him *unhandy* at the task. The sign explained, in Vietnamese as well as English, that he'd lost his hands to a land-mine he'd been attempting to deactivate, and wouldn't I like to donate a few piasters to his living costs? Well, I've been the target of many, many persuasive panhandling pitches, before and since. Every now and then, one seems genuine. I dug my wallet out of my back pocket. Fumbled out some piasters. Not enough. Fumbled out *all* my piasters. It probably amounted to fifteen hundred or so. Four bucks, American. But, on the other hand, more than a day's wages in Saigon, in 1971. I proffered the bills. The guy sort-of thrust out his chest, as if offering his shirt pocket, so I stuffed the bills in there. He smiled broadly, said "*cảm ơn ông vui lòng*," which meant "thank you very much" or "thank you kindly," or something to that effect. He hopped out and walked away.

Ten or fifteen more minutes and here came Miss Mai. I dismounted and helped her in. Our eyes met. There did not seem to be joy in hers. I went around my side, hopped in, fired it up. "How did it go?" I asked.

"Maybe they have two or three more month."

"Well, *chi* Mai, that's not so—"

"Not at Joint Command! Other place!"

In a few weeks, she and I would cease spending nine or ten hours a day in close proximity. I had put that entire likelihood outside of my sense of the feasible. I drove with meticulous precision, but my secret objective was to make our drive together back to Joint Command last a hundred years. Obviously, it didn't work.

Mai had about three weeks until her last day. I had about three months. There was, however, a sneaky little wrinkle to be found in taking one's DEROS (Date of Estimated Return from OverSeas) lying down. Add it up. Day Zero: inducted. Then eight weeks of Basic Training. Two weeks of leave. Nine weeks of Intelligence School. Two more weeks of leave. Twelve months combat-duty in Viet Nam. Doing the arithmetic? That added up to something approaching eighteen months. A draftee's commitment was two years – twenty-four months. The reassignment break-even point for the Army was five months. In other words, if you took that Freedom Bird on back to the USofA on your DEROS date, you'd have enough commitment left to make it worthwhile to reassign you. Off you'd go to Fort Dismal, Arkansaw, to spend every day up until the very last smidge of your draftee obligation peeling spuds or scrubbing latrines, fancy-ass Ninety-Six Bravo training notwithstanding. Less than five months at DEROS, they'd just cut you loose, and you were a civilian again, nevermore to wear the green. Well so the solution, if you could call it that, was to *volunteer to serve a couple extra months in Viet Nam!*

Oh my did that necessity go down hard! Still, nearly everyone did a short, voluntary re-up. Looked *great* on the enlistment-officers' datasheets. Damned hard to explain to the wives and sweethearts – may they never meet – back home. Well so I was on the very brink of putting in my paperwork to extend my tour when a buddy of mine in Battalion Admin broke his solemn Oath of Omerta and delivered up a top-secret confidence.

"Don't do it!" he warned me. "There's an Army-wide deal in the works that anyone having ten and a half months in-country, can *opt-out!*"

"What's that mean, opt-out?"

"*Go home*, asshole!" And no stateside reassignment! Only thing you'll sacrifice is maybe a month or two of GI college benefits, and you've already got a BS so what the Hell!"

"It all sounds like a red herring...." I scoffed.

"No! It's for sure! I've seen the orders! But—"

"But what?"

"But if you've already submitted an extension request, they

won't let you rescind it! It'll be okayed so some other jackass can go home six weeks early and leave you hanging around here."

There was only one thing I would consider hanging around for. And she was going to be made scarce in about two more weeks. Against my better judgment, I let my buddy's crock of crap convince me. I held off on submitting my extension request.

Imagine my surprise when five days later a Major from somewhere on up the chain of command came into the OB Element and asked, "Who'd like to bump their DEROS date six weeks?" That would get me on an eastbound airplane about mid-February. I nearly dislocated my shoulder getting my hand up in the air and waving it around.

19

Good-Bye

Inevitably the day came, Mai's last day on the job at Joint Command. The clock hands spun like game-spinners, and the hours flew away into oblivion. Approaching four o'clock. I could not speak. I could not move. Scarcely could I breathe. I pretended to do work that didn't really need doing. Then Specialist Marsden got up and took his leave, heading off to God-knows-where. Only Sergeant Timmons left in the office, atonally humming a Doors tune with his headset clapped over his ears. And Mai, of course…and me. Then Timmons had a look at the clock, snapped off his tapedeck, cavalierly tossed his headset into a drawer, and headed out the door. She and I were alone. There were perhaps ten minutes left of that final, ultimate day.

Mai peeked into the hallway. No one out there. Gently, she closed the Edit Office door. That door was never closed – ever! I stood and came around the front of my desk, leaned casually against its comfortless edge. She glided across the floor in that graceful way she had, and stood a handful of inches from me, looking up into my face with those sweet, searching brown eyes. Words deserted both of us. But I knew – *I knew!* – she had prepped herself for this moment, at home, with her notepad and her Vietnamese/English Dictionary, like she always did when she had something important to tell me. She took my hand. Like always, it was as if four thousand volts of cosmic-ray energy flowed into my hand from her slim fingertips. "I don't want to leave you," she told me, slowly and with great, precise articulation, and I knew these six short words were the speech she'd memorized, the all-encompassing thought that told me all that was in her heart. Her voice was soft and low, but it was clear she was at the ragged edge of control.

"Mai…" I heard myself respond. "Mai…If I were not married to another woman, *I would never leave you!*" It was probably too complex a sentence for her limited English to process, but I could see she understood.

149

Then she came into my arms. Her lips found mine. The kiss was like none other, like no kiss I have ever known, before or since…perhaps like no kiss in the history of humankind. Mai conveyed a lifetime – a dozen lifetimes! – of passion and tenderness and unalloyed love in the infinite twenty seconds of that kiss, because she knew it was all we were going to have, ever. I don't know how or where she learned the skill of it. Forty years gone, and I can close my eyes and taste her kiss. Feel her arms gently around me. Experience her slim, lovely body pressing softly against me. Up until that moment, there had been no outright intimate contact like that between us, nothing at all because we had stalwartly been so chaste, so guarded, and yet there had been *nothing but* dear, loving intimacy for all those months. Mai's kiss was the entire consummation of our love.

We drew apart. Our eyes were filled with tears, hers and mine. Both of us knew and dreaded what had to come next.

-*-*-*-

In a terrible flash of insight I knew it could not end like this! I seized her by the upper arms, my fingers pressing painfully into her tender flesh. "Mai…" I demanded. "Tell me truly -- *Do you love me?*"

This was the quintessential question. All this time, we had flirted with this notion, tasted it perhaps, but avoided venturing unequivocally onto this quaking, treacherous ground. I dreaded that her sense of what was right, her instinct for *what had to be*, would keep her from answering me truthfully. But in the end, she did not have the strength to let restraint prevail against the emotion she felt. She dropped her eyes to the floor. I could see little shudders running through her, feel her trembling in my gripping hands. When she looked up into my face, tears slid from the corners of her beautiful, beautiful eyes and traced shameful lines down her cheeks, dripped off her chin. Then she answered me with a chilling firmness and certainty.

"Yes! All my heart, I love you! LOVE you! No one else, forever!" she wept desperately.

I'm sure my mouth fell open in a gape of complete amazement. Then she uttered my name in that screwy way of hers that was so endearing. "Do you love *me? Do you?*" she asked.

YesyesyesYES! How could I tell her more clearly? Show her? I embraced her and we hugged, then we kissed, then we hugged some more, then we were laughing, quietly and hysterically, tears of joy streaming, conscious that if we made too much of a scene, the door would fly open and one of the unit's Master-Sergeants would be standing there, or perhaps Colonel Childers himself…and there would be tall explaining to do.

"What we can do?" she asked. Ah yes. A large question. What are we going to do? My mind whirled a hundred times its usual best-speed. "I'll be going back home in three weeks, when my DEROS comes up. My enlistment will be over when I get to the States. I'll be out of the Army! Mai, it won't be easy but I will just have to tell Elle that she'll need to give me my freedom…that I have never betrayed our promises, but I have fallen deeply in love with another woman, and she and I cannot succeed in having any further life together. Then I will come for you. I don't know how. Wait for me…we'll be together. I swear to you! My parents will help us get you travel papers, a visa. We'll marry…you *will* marry me, won't you? Oh Love! Oh Beloved!" I don't suppose she understood much of that, and I was making it up as I went, but her eyes were alight with joy and she was nodding her affirmation and smiling nonstop.

And so it happened. In a few months, I was a free man in all respects. I was on an airplane, bound westward across the broad Pacific Ocean toward the woman I'd found by accident on the other side of the world, frantically in love, two passports in my coat pocket, mine and hers, along with visas and tickets and traveler's checks and clearance documents, ready to

151

20

The Truth

Shit. Shitshitshitshit! It's all lies. I've lied like that to myself for forty years, and now I'm lying to you. Back up to that little line of stars and dashes a few paragraphs back. That's the place where I start lying, where I always commence making up the story of *what should have been.* I've been doing it for four decades now. I indulge in this fantasy when I'm trying to fall asleep, but cannot. I make up this little scripted dialogue when I'm in the car alone, driving tedious, long miles across empty country. I act out this little dramatic production when I've drunk too much, and the balm of drink fails to bring forgetfulness and brings remembrance instead. But it did not go like that at all. Here's how it *really* went:

We drew apart. Our eyes were filled with tears, hers and mine. Both of us knew and dreaded what had to come next. She uttered my name in that screwy way of hers that was so endearing. It was the last time -- save one -- I would ever again hear her speak my name. "Good-Bye," she added in a desperate whisper. There was no implication of "See ya later!" like these words sometime suggest when spoken casually by the American-born...it was good-bye, plain and simple, the end, gone forever, the final parting.

"Good-Bye, Mai" I managed to choke out in answer. Then, quieter still, "Good-Bye, my Love"...but I don't think she heard that second farewell.

She was gone.

I held my face in my hands and wept.

21

What I Have Missed

I have never seen Miss Mai again. Except whenever I close my eyes. Often, when I dream, she comes to me. When I hear that particular song I already told you about, her face swims into my vision. I cannot hear that song, no matter what the circumstances, without a tear or two, and I've had to become adept at hiding them. I have four photographs that I occasionally take out of my lockbox of deeds and wills and private papers, or out of my wallet. I spend some quiet minutes gazing at these aging images of her forever-young visage. Then I lock them away again. Sometimes a whole day manages to get past me without my thinking about her, but surely not above once or twice in every thousand days I contrive to go on living.

I will never feel the intimate pressure of her arm through mine as we sit next to each other on a plane, its engines running-up for takeoff to some far place we are going on holiday together…a pressure that tells me the plane can crash in a fiery ball at the end of this runway if it cares to, but it will not matter because we are *together*, now and forever. I will never hear her little indrawn gasp of delight when the curtain goes up on the staging of a Puccini opera and the soprano, bejeweled and splendidly gowned, begins her aria. I will never see her magic, childlike smile of spontaneous joy over some trivial gift or kindness. I will never taste the mystic, Asian-spiced sweetness of her kiss, although I still cling to the honey-mouthed taste of that single magical kiss we shared in January of 1972. I will never experience the all-encompassing avalanche of sweet sensations when I've succeeded in taking her to the limits of feminine ecstasy, and her climactic paroxysm confirms that there is, in point of fact, a time for us. I'll never share any of those blissful moments with her. But I will love her forever.

22

Reflections on a Black Granite Wall

S o ended my Viet Nam experience. Do I strive to hold myself up to comparison with those hundreds of thousands of my comrades who crept terrified and miserable through filth and jungles and elephant-grass, faced a hundred kinds of death and pain from enemy mortars, automatic weapon-fire, booby traps, disease and worse, whose Viet Nam experiences were something far other than what I've told you about here? No, of course not, and I've been careful all these years to never forget the difference, and always remember to thank whatever Almighty there might have been, sheltering me from far worse than what I experienced personally. I've tried to see things from the proper point-of-view, and not to forget to look at the other side of the paper. I confess to carrying an oversized, secret morsel of mortification that my Viet Nam tour was mostly free from hazard and fear, and that all I suffered was a wounded heart. It helps my troubled conscience very little to note that for every combat soldier, boots on the muddy ground, there were eight or ten troops in support roles, fairly removed from risk, just like me. As you have seen, I've refrained from trying to write about the horrible aspects of the Viet Nam War, and I've stuck to what I know...as all writers are advised to do.

Times of war affect us all, however...affect us in our minds and our souls, all of us. All the civilians in every involved nation -- American, South Vietnamese, North Vietnamese. All the GIs, and all the ARVNs, and all the NVA, and all the Viet Cong. I would never pretend to have been unaffected myself. The doleful impact of all that savagery and violence and death of those years even extends to all the simple, innocent souls like those of twenty-two-year-old typists.

In our nation's capital, back in 1982 they put up a memorial to all the young men, dead before their time in Viet Nam. Black granite panels, starting out barely knee-high but climbing at the vee-shaped monument's apex to more than ten feet in height. Two long wings, totaling around 500 feet in length.   Fifty-eight thousand two hundred seventy-two names.   One time a few years after the Memorial was dedicated, my older brother (who did not serve in the military) pointed out to me that the wall did not memorialize ALL the young men who died in the Viet Nam War. Nor the old men, nor the women, nor the children, nor the babies. He was speaking, of course, of the Vietnamese fatalities, military and civilian, South and North.   And the Laotian fatalities, and the Cambodian fatalities.   I don't think he was trying to belittle the memories of the American servicemen who died…he was just trying to point out that there was another side to the paper on which *our* dead veterans were listed.   I was a little scandalized by his statement.   Include our *enemies* in the reckoning of the dead? Well, they are just as dead, he suggested. And it's doubtful that each of them cherished life or held to worthwhile values any the less than each of us.   The way my brother saw it, a tourist on the Capitol Mall in Washington D.C. ought to step back about two hundred yards from the Veteran's Memorial Wall, and look out over the top of it, and visualize in his imagination a second wall a couple hundred yards beyond the black granite one.   Only if that second wall were *half a mile* long and *fifty* feet high would it have room for the names of all the Asian dead.   Perhaps, my brother offered, that's the larger, more-clement point-of-view one ought to take, when contemplating those killed in warfare: don't stop contemplating until you've contemplated them *all*.

When they mustered me out, back in Alameda, California, they took back almost all my issue of jungle fatigues, my dress khakis, my Viet Nam boots with their pungi-stake-proof soles.   They issued me a natty dress-green uniform, so I'd look Class-A on that civilian plane-ride home, and when I walked down a jetway in a stateside hometown somewhere, to be embraced by my parents or my wife or my girlfriend.   No, I won't say that stupid punchline again.

That's what I did.   Elle had convinced Airport Security she was vision-impaired, so they'd let her bring Reddy right on up into the arrival concourse in the Portland airport.   He went nuts when he got a sniff of me from fifty feet away. When we got home to Elle's shabby trailer, I took that Class-A uniform off and hung it in the closet. It has hung in a succession of closets since that day, more than forty years ago. I've never worn it again. Of course, I'd never get back into it these days.

Elle and I did all right for a long time. I hid the scars on my heart. Whatever Elle might have known or suspected, she never spoke about it. I didn't try to write Mai. There hardly seemed to be a point...it would just keep the heart-scars open and suppurating. Then, when Vietnamization emerged as the fiasco it was and the North Vietnamese and Viet Cong started really rolling southward, as they'd claimed they would for the last twenty years, it seemed to me that what Miss Tuoi Mai needed *least of all* was a nice pen-pal in the United States who'd once been a Ninety-Six Bravo in the US Army's Joint Intelligence Command Center, Saigon, VN. My worst nightmare was of that sweet, guileless, beautiful girl stood up against a wall and being hosed-down by a squad of AK47-wielding NVA. Only slightly less gruesome, a sentence in prison, or a long stint in a "re-education" facility. I stayed out of her life for those reasons, and other reasons too convoluted to enunciate.

Elle and I did all right for a long time. In 1975, as April drew to a close, at exactly the time of the Fall of Saigon, practically to the day, we got cranking on making a baby. Hot sex, three times a day, simultaneous climaxes every time, best synchronicity we ever, ever accomplished. The result, conceived with all that love and passion, was my daughter, the light of my life, grown now into a woman of such remarkable loveliness and quirky brilliance that in many ways she reminds me of Tuoi Mai.

And then Elle and I stopped doing so all right. It happened gradually and there's no one to blame. Was I changed? Damaged? Tainted, by Viet Nam? Hell, we *all* were! Those of us who went, those of us who stayed at home. Was there blame to cast on my fierce, intense, albeit mostly unrequited love for Mai? I don't even know the answer to that one. After twenty years of marriage, Elle and I managed our parting with a modicum of civility.

There were a few years of solitude for me, at least in terms of a lover, a life partner. They weren't so terribly bad. Didn't kill me, so must have made me stronger. I grew a lot during that time. Got a Master's Degree in Education and went into schoolteaching. Algebra, computer science, chemistry, physics at the high-school level. Please don't ask me why…it's tougher than Basic Training! Eventually, in a pure stroke of serendipity, I met Dee.

Dee has a tranquil and calming personality. Dee flashes brightness and intelligence but is self-effacing, almost to a fault. Dee moves with grace – once I told her she glides like an otter, and she found that memorable…no one had ever told her such a thing. Dee has dark hair, clinging around her skull like a fragrant cap. Quirky sense of humor. Tendency to mispronounce things in the most endearing fashion…just, not my name. Dee's sense of style is unique and immaculate. Dee looks wonderful in floaty, silken garments. Dee's skin is impeccably flawless save for a dusting of freckles, and in hue is a pale, subtle café-au-lait that doesn't tan well in the sunshine. Dee is not Vietnamese, but she transcends nationality. I did not consciously choose Dee because of her resemblances to Mai…that would have been obsessive and unlikely to produce much in the way of satisfaction for either of us. And anyway, we unhesitatingly chose each other, in the first few weeks of our acquaintance. But perhaps – no, almost certainly! – I found myself drawn to some of the same qualities that made me fall so desperately in love with Tuoi Mai, forty years ago.

Have I ever tried to relocate Mai? I have, with very little success. It is so painful to thrash through those vain attempts that have failed to lead me to any kind of closure. Once, not long ago, I placed a "singles" ad on a website where it would be seen by some of those Vietnamese women I witnessed weeping over the fate of a star-crossed pair of imaginary Italian-Renaissance teenagers who'd been invented by an Elizabethan hack playwright. If that degree of sentimentality could not be enlisted to help me find Mai, I was much mistaken. Several very kindhearted individuals in Ho Chi Minh City – which is what they are calling Saigon these days – did some amateur sleuthing in the vicinity of 92 Gia Long Street, District 1, HCMC. They interviewed old-time residents.

Recollections were dim. One oldster seemed to remember someone named Mai who would have been the correct age and looked something like her hauntingly-beautiful portrait from age nineteen. But she was dead. Passed away sometime in the spring of 2003, as he recalled. I didn't receive this tentative information until the spring of 2012. There is no indisputable verification of this in the excellently-managed death-records archive of HCMC, so there is every possibility Tuoi Mai lives to this day.

Has her life been good? Has she been happy? Fulfilled? Did she suffer at the hands of the North Vietnamese when the South fell? Excuse me…the proper term is "underwent reunification." Did she marry? Bear children? Did she attempt to flee in the dismal, dangerous boatborne exodus of the early 80's, and languish in an internment camp for endless months? Did she return to Dalat, her birthplace? Or did she stick it out in Saigon, and continue her drive for English fluency? Does she remember me? Love me still? Does she wear that ring of golden dolphins? So many questions, so many.

One night I lay asleep not five inches away from my softly slumbering wife Dee. I was jolted awake at three in the morning in a pitch-dark bedroom. Someone had called my name. Twice, in a clear, distinct voice. The voice was unmistakable, because the pronunciation of my name, five simple letters, two simple syllables, no weird diphthongs or aberrant vowel pronunciations, could only have been mangled so ditzily by one person ever in the history of human speech, and that person is Tuoi Mai, and it was the last time I have ever heard her say my name.

This happened sometime in the spring of 2003.

In the end, it comes down to only a very simple wish, the likelihood of satisfaction for which my skeptical spirit holds very little hope. If there were to exist a mystic pathway by which one person's soul, earnestly motivated by yearning, undying bonds of fondness, could somehow connect with the soul of another, though she may live far away in an unknown place…or have vanished beyond this worldly life altogether…I would beg to say only these following words so that my long-ago lost love may hear them in her heart. And if through my ignorance or faulty research I've made errors, I would joyfully and humbly receive her lessoning in the right of it as regards the spelling:

Tôi yêu chi Mãi

OTHER NOVELS BY LEWIS MACLEOD

Twenty-One Forty-Seven – Book One of 'THE SOLAE' series

In the year 2147, humankind has begun to exceed the critical planetary ecological tipping-point in many frightening ways. Global population exceeds nine billion souls. Unspoiled areas on every continent are shrunken, their wildlife depleted. Poverty is rife in every nation. Petroleum reserves worldwide are nearly exhausted. Sources of water for domestic and agricultural use are severely overtaxed. Air quality has never been so compromised. Still, there is hope. Technology has led to stunning advances, and man's ventures into space have proceeded spectacularly. A new faith -- that of the Solae -- has arisen from the urban slums of South America, promising a new and vital view on human interactions. Perhaps humanity's future is not so grim after all.

On 15 September, in the year Twenty-One Forty-Seven, all that changes

The Solae – Book Two of 'THE SOLAE' series

It is nearly a thousand years beyond the present day. The globe and the human race are slowly recovering from the horrors of a devastating war and plague that occurred in the year 2147. Humanity lives simply, without the technologies of today, for the net of industry, medicine, and science was shattered beyond recovery by the tribulations of that war. Small villages of farmers and herdsmen cluster against the flank of the mountains once known as the Rockies. On the High Plains, a few fiercely protective bands of nomads make their seasonal migrations, practicing their arts and trades with whatever peaceable folk they encounter. Deep in a mountain fastness dwells a secretive sect, whose avowed purpose is to collect and safeguard scraps of scientific knowledge that survived the Laser War...safeguard this knowledge until the Deserving One their faith prophesies will come forward to receive this store of wisdom. And always, bringing terror and death as their ally, the bands of pitiless, thieving murderers wander this cold and terrible world, marauders known by all men as ULTS.

...But a change is about to come upon this savage world.

Solae Inheritor – Book Three of 'THE SOLAE' series

The Union of Eriss has grown and consolidated for more than a hundred years since its founding in the famine-depleted High Plains of the continent. To the east, an implacable enemy stirs: the Atlan Empire, warlike, aggressive, greedy for land, for power and for slaves. The Union is vigorous and vital, but not without its difficulties: one-third of its population are Ults, restless descendants of a conquered race of one-time wildland brigands and marauders on whom the veneer of Erissard civilization lies thin and uneasy. It is the special task of the House of Eriss, descendants of Old Salin lineage, to defend the Union. But the family's elder, the Domin Therisam, is aged, weak and vacillating. It is good fortune that his eldest son and proxy Jericharek is a man of fierce determination, although his character is flawed by the hateful evil of bigotry directed toward the Ultish populace. Jeri's younger brother Mairhos, although not born into leadership, has a gentler spirit and a keen sense of duty and honor. He heeds the call to serve his nation in less-celebrated ways. But another call also rises in his heart: the impassioned love of a girl from the poorer classes of Pikemond City. Karil Feros is innocent, beautiful, skilled, fearless, and kind of heart, but, may the Sacred Solae pity Mairhos, Karil is one thing more.

Karil is Ult.

Solae Redeemer – Book Four of 'THE SOLAE' series

In the months following the defeat of the Atlan Empire, many citizens of the Erissard Union and its allies remained scattered by the dislocations of war. Karil Feros, Ultish paramour of the High Domin of Eriss himself, waits for her lover in the wilderness reaches of the Sulfur Basin, along with the wives, children and oldsters of her Brisach Ult forbears. The Basin is an ancient volcanic caldera, known in earlier times as the Yellowstone. There is a cataclysmic eruption, as geologists have been predicting since the nineteenth century a.d. By a miracle, Karil and her cousin Rechalas are temporarily absent on a diplomatic mission westward. Their survival is chancy and unlikely, and Mairhos has scant effort to spare in their rescue. But with help and great good fortune, he manages.

...Only, it takes him eight years to find Karil.

20099552R00094

Made in the USA
San Bernardino, CA
26 March 2015